ALTERNATIVE TO THE PENTAGON

ALTERNATIVE TO THE PENTAGON

Nonviolent Methods of Defending a Nation

Franklin Zahn

FOR
Fellowship of Reconciliation

Fellowship Publications
Nyack, New York

Fellowship Publications is a part of the Fellowship of Reconciliation (FOR), an international, spiritually-based network of people committed to active nonviolence as a means of personal, social, and political change. For eight decades, the FOR has worked against militarism, war, and injustice, seeking a just and peaceful world community, with full dignity and freedom for every human being.

This book was designed and printed by Celo Book Production Service, 346 Seven Mile Ridge Road, Burnsville, North Carolina 28714.

To order this book directly from the publisher, add $2.75 to the price for the first copy, 75¢ for each additional copy. Send check or money order to: Fellowship Publications, P.O. Box 271, Nyack, NY 10960.

Cover photo: The nuclear submarine USS *Haddo* cuts through symbolic blockade by 150 small craft in Auckland Harbor, New Zealand, January, 1979. *Photo by Chris Cooper. (courtesy American Friends Service Committee.)*

Printed on recycled paper, using mostly soy-based ink.

ISBN 0-911810-80-3
Library of Congress Catalog Card Number 96-84558

Printed in the United States of America.

Contents

List of Illustrations . . . vii
Preface . . . ix
Acknowledgments . . . xiii
1 Reasons for revolutionizing our defense philosophy . . . 1
2 Terminologies; Martin Luther King, Jr.'s six characteristics of nonviolent action . . . 15
3 Bertrand Russell's civilian defense proposals; Jessie Wallace Hughan . . . 19
4 Scenario: Superpower Axis X invades disarmed U.S. . . . 23
5 Scenario: Resisters block streets and hold ground . . . 41
6 Scenario: Pressure placed on invading army . . . 61
7 Historical accounts of unarmed resistance . . . 71
Photo section . . . 89
8 Scenario: Invaders plan capture of Fort Knox . . . 103
9 Scenario: Tanks employ scare tactics . . . 121
10 Scenario: Tanks advance and resisters employ nonviolent action . . . 133
11 Scenario: Fort Knox blasted open and counterinvaded . . . 147
Conclusion . . . 157
Notes . . . 159
Index . . . 163
About the Author . . . 173

List of Illustrations

A-1. U.S. Federal Budget for 1997 2

A-2. The Government's view of the Federal budget 3

B. Map of New York Harbor 28

C. Diagram of troopship *Queen Elizabeth 2* being pulled away from shore by blockading vessels 39

D. Map of Eastern Virginia, showing point of resistance to invasion 104

E. Water jet resisters (close-up) 126

F. Water jet resisters (from above) 127

All photographs can be found on pp. 89–101.

Preface

Let us imagine a weaker nation in an unequal struggle for its freedom from control by a powerful one. A description of the two nations may sound familiar: The weaker is tropical, underdeveloped, with a low standard of living. Most of its dark-skinned citizens are agriculturists. The dominant nation, a Western industrialized culture, has warships and military bases circling the globe. It has troops and superior weaponry on the distant soil of the less developed country.

Let us also suppose that after the failure of all their attempts to reach a negotiated settlement, the occupied people finally decide to fight with what inferior weapons they have. At least their war for independence will be fought on familiar home ground, without the thousands of miles of supply lines that will be needed by the invader. They may know from history of successes of weaker armies under similar circumstances — the American Revolution, for example. So they take up arms to drive out the aggressive foreigners, prepared to pay in blood and lives the heavy price of freedom.

But let us alternatively suppose that the people decide instead to wage their struggle entirely by non-cooperation and nonviolent resistance, discarding all reliance on weapons. Let us assume, as previously, all attempts to negotiate a peaceful resolution with the oppressor have failed, the only difference being that the last resort chosen was not a violent struggle but a nonviolent one.

If the two scenarios are hypothetical, we can only speculate on their outcomes. If the reader has already thought of India and Great Britain in the second scenario, let us examine that actual result. The total number of Indian lives lost from the beginning of their nonviolent campaign is estimated to have been some eight thousand. Although many British soldiers died in previous armed revolts, none died in the nonviolent campaign itself.

Returning to the first case in which violence was chosen, let us take the actual example of the United States and Vietnam — another pair of countries fitting the description of a superior Western power on the soil of a weaker third-world nation. The number of Vietnamese lives lost in that struggle is estimated to have been 1,900,000 — or 237 times more fatalities than in India. (The United States lost fifty-five thousand.)

The contrast in weaker nation losses is even greater when populations are considered. In North and South Vietnam in 1972–73, roughly the period when U.S. troops were pulling out, the total population was 41,253,000, which calculates to be one Vietnamese death for every 21 people. India's population, in its census prior to 1947 independence, was 388,997,955, which means only one Indian died for every 48,624 people. The way of *satyagraha*, or "truth force" as Gandhi called it, used in India's struggle, was spectacularly successful compared with the violence used in Vietnam if only on a cost-in-lives basis.

Added to this fatalities basis of comparison should be of course the wounded and the damage to property. The pictures of destroyed Vietnamese villages, defoliated forests, shell-holed farms, and rubbled cities were familiar to anyone who followed the news. To this day, unexploded bombs and artillery shells continue to kill and wound farmers. By contrast, India at the time of liberation had suffered almost no property damage.

Only in duration were the two struggles similar. U.S. forces were in Vietnam from 1961 to 1975. Successors to the defeated French, in earlier stages they were "advisors" to U.S.-financed South Vietnamese troops. India's first nonviolent action with definite implications for independence was the 1930 Salt Tax Campaign. Later actions were interspersed with long periods of negotiations until independence was finally granted in 1947. We could compare fourteen years of Vietnam's violent war with seventeen for India's nonviolent campaign.

In view of Vietnam's tremendous losses, as well as countless numbers of other such wars, one wonders why any oppressed country would resort to ordinary warfare without first thoroughly considering some form of nonviolent alternative. Admittedly there were tremendous differences between the two situations; all that is claimed here is that both fitted our original hypotheticals.

One cliché, especially before the example of Martin Luther King, Jr., was that mass *satyagraha* worked in India because the British are very humane. Such a view would receive little acceptance by the Irish after their centuries of struggle with Britain. Ironically, it was the 1919 British massacre at Amritsar which finally decided Gandhi to abandon negotiations and adopt nonviolent resistance. In that atrocity riflemen fired into a trapped assembly of unarmed Indians, killing 379. Three Englishmen had been murdered, and General Dyer wanted to teach the inhabitants a lesson. After his hearing he was censured by other Britons but never punished. As late as 1942 Gandhi received a report of a British soldier throwing a refugee child under a train.

It is often forgotten that Gandhi's first successes with nonviolent resistance were in South Africa during the struggle between Indians and the repressive Boer government. More will be said later about the Sharpeville massacre in that nation.

The purpose of this book is to show how the method used by Gandhi, and later by Martin Luther King, Jr., could be used successfully by the United States to repel any powerful invading force. Not only would the cost saved in lives and property be considerable, but the country would go a long way toward rebuilding its peacetime economy. Instead of distinguishing itself as the world's most powerful supercop, pressuring weaker nations by armed intervention or threat of it, the U.S. could become an eminent senior partner. New friends around the globe would be eager to deal with a superpower that tried less to dominate and more to cooperate. And the example of total self-disarmament by the most powerful of militarized nations could well be a first step leading to similar renunciations and a world free of war.

Acknowledgments

The following read this book in preparation and made useful comments and suggestions: Paul Anders, Melvin Beckman, and Philip Helms of the Civilian-Based Defense Association; an anonymous Lt. General of the United States Army; David Hartsough, Executive Director, *Peacekeepers*; Maj. Emerson Pittman, United States Air Force; Ronan Reynolds, powerplant mechanical engineer.

The City of New York and Con Edison supplied information about public utilities, The United States Treasury Department about the Depository at Fort Knox, and Cunard Line about the *Queen Elizabeth II*.

Because suggestions of those who read earlier unpublished fictional versions have been used in the scenario portions of this final book, it seems proper their names and positions at the time also be included. I begin with A.J. Muste, formerly with the Fellowship of Reconciliation and later with the War Resisters' League; James Bristol and Stephen Cary, Peace Education Division of the American Friends Service Committee; Markley Morris, peace writer; Albert Bigelow and George Willoughby of the nuclear protest boat *Golden Rule*; Glenn Smiley, the Fellowship of Reconciliation; Ferner Nuhn, Quaker writer; Theodore Olsen, nonviolent activist, Upland Institute; John Stoner, Mennonite leader, New Call to Peacemaking; Vladimir Ulitin, Russian engineer; Richard Deats, the Fellowship of Reconciliation, (and overseeing publication of this ultimate version); Dennis Hartzel, Virginia botanist; Paul Encimer, editor of *The Peacemaker*; Dan Merrit and Steve Smith, both Gandhian scholars and professors at Claremont McKenna College and University of La Verne, respectively, Aimee Elsbee, Quaker mother; Robert Holmes, philosopher and author; and Katherine Morseberger, Quaker writer.

1

Reasons for Revolutionizing Our Defense Philosophy

Of the many problems facing people in the United States[1] in the last decade of the twentieth century — the economy, street violence, discrimination based on race, gender, and sexual-orientation, health care, the AIDS epidemic, pollution, environmental devastation, dwindling natural resources — the economy and endemic violence probably directly affect the largest numbers. If it were not for the troubled economy, there would be more money for alleviating the poverty which is so much a part of crime and discrimination, for finding a cure for AIDS, for cleaning up the environment, and for providing better health care.

Military spending is a major villain in this troubled economy; the borrowing and high taxes for the Pentagon could be largely eliminated by substituting an alternative form of national defense. This substitution could play a direct part in lessening the depletion of the world's resources, in decreasing pollution, and indirectly in reducing street violence.

Few taxpayers are aware of how much the United States spends on the military; that in 1993 its $277.1 billion budget was more than that of the next ten highest countries combined. The pie chart (Figure A) for the 1997 projected budget shows the Department of Defense portion to be only twenty-two percent. But this pie includes Social Security and

The United States Federal Budget for Fiscal Year 1997

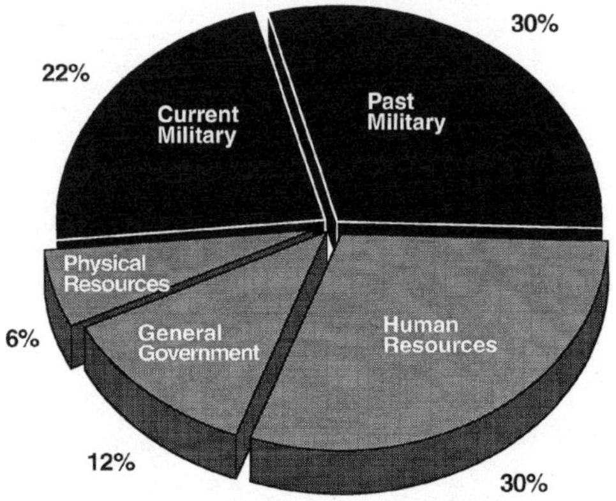

How These Figures Were Determined

War Resisters League creates these flyers each year after the President has presented the budget. This year, however, the 1996 budget process is not yet finished, and President Clinton has offered only a skeletal 1997 budget. Our figures are 1997 projections as reported in the Budget of the United States Government, Fiscal Year 1996. They do not reflect the many changes Congress is still making to the current year budget and the future impact of those changes. One thing we know: the military budget is Congress's "sacred cow."

The percentages are Federal Funds, calculated after removing Trust Funds (such as Social Security), which are raised and spent separately from income taxes. What you pay (or don't pay) on April 15 goes only to the Federal Funds portion of the budget. The government practice of combining Trust and Federal Funds (the so-called "Unified Budget") began in the 1960's during the Vietnam War. The government presentation makes the human needs portion of the budget seem larger and the military portion smaller. "Current military" spending adds together money allocated for the Department of Defense ($247 billion) plus the "defense" portion from other parts of the budget. Spending on nuclear weapons (without their delivery systems) amounts to about 1% of the total budget. "Past military" is represented by veterans' benefits plus 80% of the interest on the national debt. If there had been no military spending, most (if not all) of the national debt would have been eliminated. Analysts differ on how much of the debt stems from the military; estimates range from 50% to 100%. We felt that 80% may even be conservative.

(Charts and information prepared by the War Resisters League)

Figure A. Part 1.

22% Current Military—$286 Billion
(Military Personnel $67B, Retired Pay $13B. Operation and Maintenance $90B, Family Housing $4B, Procurement $46B, Research and Development $33B, Construction $5B, DoE Nuclear Weapons $10B, NASA 50% $7B, Coast Guard $4B, plus CIA, President's Funds. International Security Assistance, FEMA.)

30% Past Military—$377 Billion
Veterans Benefits $39B. Interest on National Debt (80% estimated to be created by military spending) $338B.

30% Human Resources—$381 Billion
(Education, Health and Human Services, HUD housing subsidies, Food Stamps, Labor Department.)

12% General Government—$156 Billion
(Government, Justice Department, International Affairs, Peace Corps, 20% interest on national debt, civilian portion of NASA.)

6% Physical Resources—$74 Billion
(Includes Agriculture, Commerce, Energy, HUD administration/community development, Interior Department, Transportation, Environmental Protection.)

100% Total Federal Funds–$1.274 Trillion

U.S. Military Budget

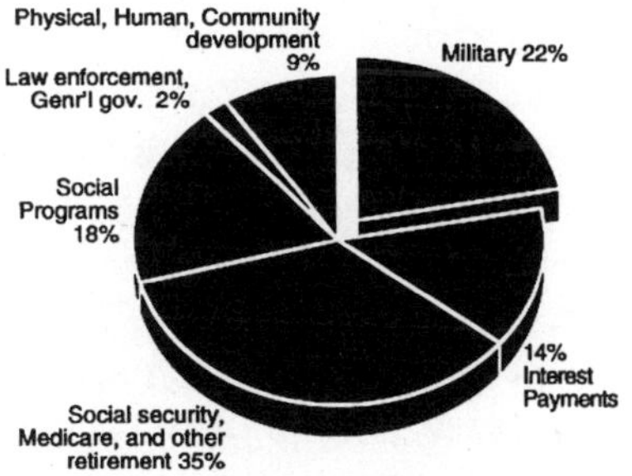

The Government Deception

The pie chart below is the Administration's view of the budget (and similar to the figures you'll see in your IRS booklet or the media). This is a distortion of how our income tax dollars are spent because it includes Trust Funds (e.g., Social Security) and buries the expenses of past military spending in nonmilitary parts of the pie. For a more accurate representation of how your Federal income tax dollar is really spent, see the large chart *(previous page).*

Figure A. Part 2.

other trust funds which, if properly left out, make the Department of Defense (DOD) budget a higher percentage of income and excise taxes. If to this we add the costs of past wars, including interest on the war-created portion of the national debt, as well as veterans' benefits, the total for war purposes rises to roughly *one-half of the income tax dollar,* depending on the percentage of the debt assumed to be war-created.

The humanitarian cost of our enormous annual military expenditures was well stated by Dwight Eisenhower, a Republican president who was also a former general: "Every gun that is made, every warship launched, every rocket fired signifies, in the final sense, a theft from those who hunger and are not fed, those who are cold and not clothed. This world in arms is not spending money alone. It is spending the sweat of its laborers, the genius of its scientists, the hopes of its children."[2]

Less than one-tenth of the current military budget, or $28 billion (according to *War Watch,* December, 1993 of "Out Now") would lift every person in the United States above the poverty line for one year. But this "theft" goes far beyond affecting only the poor; because of its inherent inflationary nature, military spending hurts every consumer. As British economist Barbara Ward explained: "Since no goods are made by the military industry to offset the wages it creates, arms spending is . . . the most inflationary of all expenditures."

In theory, a balanced market economy could raise taxes to prevent inflation. But political slogans of "no new taxes" — which cleverly direct attention away from the bad old ones — have resulted instead in cutting budgets for civilian needs, raising interest rates to reduce money flow, and giving enormous profits to the war industry while going further into debt — all in the name of an adequate "defense."

Further, because the DOD has become a major consumer of civilian goods it does not provide, it is promoting both sides of the classic statement of inflation: *More* money chasing *fewer* goods. It is the biggest consumer in the United States of oil, and a major one of steel and water, competing with the public for these necessities and thus raising their price. It is not only a major owner of land but also in a sense a consumer of it, often rendering it unfit for other use, as will be mentioned later.

Again it was Eisenhower who warned of the "military-industrial complex." Seymour Melman has described these 20,000 war contractors and 100,000 subcontractors as a new "concentration of power hitherto unknown in the American experience."[3] While traditional economics tries to minimize costs and maximize profits, Melman claims the new complex maximizes costs in order to maximize government subsidies. He cites profits reported by the government's Renegotiating Board ranging from a low of fifty percent up to five hundred percent of the net worth of firms contracting with the DOD, and contrasts this with testimony of Senator Proxmire that "average profits of all manufacturing firms ranges from eighteen percent to twenty percent annually."

Melman refers to data showing that a commercially manufactured article costing a basic $100 (say a TV) would cost anywhere from $250 to $2,393 when made by a DOD contractor. In 1993 the House Government Operations Committee observed that "The Defense Department remains the captive of special interests, each promoting new, expensive programs. . . . There are few incentives to save money. . . ."[4]

The DOD at times has had a reported two thousand lobbyists testifying before Congress for new appropriations. This writer was told by his representative that lobbyists, when questioned about the need, often said such details were classified information. Employees of military industries have also been organized to lobby for new contracts.

Melman, himself a professor of industrial engineering, goes far beyond its mere profiteering in his complaint against the "complex":

> In American industry competent technology and industrial efficiency have become casualties of the war economy. This is revealed in the epidemic deteriorization of research and production capability in major (civilian) industries by the progressive inability of many firms to hold even the domestic market against foreign competition, and by the subsequent formation of capital and labor surpluses (read unemployment). . . . These results were unavoidable in the . . . relentless drive by the war-economy directorate (military-industrial-complex) to enlarge its decisive power in the name of national security.

This deteriorization is due in large measure to the emphasis on research for better weapons rather than for better and lower-priced civilian goods. In its "Competitive Strength of U.S. Industrial & Science Technology: Strategic Issues," The National Science Board states some sixty-five percent of all public research and development funding goes to military use.[5] Cassidy and Bean give a lower figure which includes private Research & Development: "Germany and Japan expend only four percent and one percent respectively of their total public and private R & D on the military. In the U.S. that figure is between thirty-five and forty percent."

Their study points to the "brain drain" from civilian to military progress in the United States as ". . . a fundamental reason Japan is ahead of the U.S. in the international marketplace. The Japanese consistently invest more of their scientific and technical resources in civilian manufacturing research. During one recent year the Japanese civilian R & D received nearly 56% more newly graduated engineers than did the same effort in the U.S."[6]

They quote Simon Ramo, former head of President Reagan's Committee on Science and Technology, on how our civilian advances trail the military, and say that we cannot continue to have so many top scientists and engineers attracted by the higher salaries, research opportunities, and latest equipment that defense contractors offer. They contend that "This has been a significant factor in the decline of the number of manufacturing jobs in the U.S. and in the production rate of goods. . . . The average annual productivity rate of growth fell . . . from 2.6% to 0.7% in manufacturing during the 1965–80 period."

The creation of jobs has often been cited as a justification for the military industry. It was recently estimated that nine million are so employed in the U.S. But many unsavory businesses also provide jobs — such as prostitution, gambling, drugs, etc. Crime itself provides jobs for police officers, detectives, lawyers, judges, prison guards, investigative reporters — the list goes on. Traffic accidents provide work for ambulance drivers, doctors, nurses, and insurance adjusters — as do tornadoes, floods, fires, and earthquakes. Whereas all these civilian jobs are in *addition* to other civilian jobs, military employment, as we have seen, is at the expense of U.S. civilian jobs lost to foreign competitors.

Further, this tradeoff of military for civilian jobs is financially a very bad bargain. The Bureau of Labor Statistics has said: "Almost any category of civilian employment will produce more work for one billion dollars than does defense production." Military production is "capital intensive," much of the dollar going for steel, aluminum and other materials, whereas, at the other end, education is the most "labor intensive," with less of its dollar going for materials and more for teacher's salaries. The Congressional Research Service has estimated that in 1993 $3 billion spent for state and local services would have made twelve thousand more jobs than if spent by the military. Thus while it is true "defense makes jobs," the whole truth is that taken overall it is responsible for a net loss.

In addition to the deleterious effects of military spending on deficit budgets, inflation, industrial competitiveness, and employment, all militaries today are enemies of world ecology. Whereas some minerals, like iron, can be reused, others like oil are simply used up. In one hour, an F-16 fighter plane consumes what a normal motorist uses in a year, an aircraft carrier in seven minutes.

Today's military products are more poisonous than ever. Less than a liter and a half of nerve gas could kill all ninety-one thousand soldiers who died from mustard gas in World War I. Plutonium is the most toxic substance ever known; when ingested, one kilogram could cause ten million lung cancers. It has a radioactive half-life of twenty-five thousand years. The Pentagon's Defense Environment Restoration Program found 17,482 toxic hot spots — places where hazardous waste posed a potential threat — in 1,855 domestic military installations. (No figures were given for bases overseas.) "The costs of cleaning up these sites are astronomical, and estimates vary widely, anywhere from $50 billion to $200 billion."[7]

In their article, "The U.S. Military's Toxic Legacy," Lenny Siegel, Gary Cohen, and Ben Goldman of the National Toxic Campaign Fund state: "The Pentagon generates more toxic waste each year than the five largest chemical companies combined."[8] We are not discussing here the high pollution and waste caused by actual warfare — such as Agent Orange in Vietnam and the burning oil wells of the Persian Gulf — but merely the ongoing by-products of training exercises, weapons testing, storage, etc.

Having seen the role the DOD plays in our troubled economy — its waste of taxes otherwise needed, its higher cost-of-living pressures, and its part in increasing unemployment — and very briefly its damaging effect on ecology and public health, we shall go on to see how it may be a factor in street violence, the other most serious problem facing U.S. citizens today.

While it is obvious that a dollar spent on the military is a dollar not spent on health, education, industrial R & D, housing, or other needs of the national economy, or that DOD's six to seven percent share of irreplaceable fossil fuels used in the U.S. is lost forever for civilian use, it is more difficult to show the relationship between military violence and civilian violence. But let us begin with what Martin Luther King, Jr. said when he announced his opposition to U.S. involvement in Vietnam:

> As I have walked among the desperate, rejected and angry young men I have told them that Molotov cocktails and rifles would not solve their problems. . . . They asked if our own nation wasn't using massive doses of violence to solve its problems, to bring about the changes it wanted. . . . I knew I could never again raise my voice against the violence of the oppressed in the ghettos without having first spoken clearly to the greatest purveyor of violence in the world today — my own government.[9]

Would King still be saying that our government is the world's *greatest* purveyor of violence? Asked in 1994 what issues she thought her father would have tackled had he not been killed, his daughter Yolanda replied:

> He talked constantly about our obsession with militarism and the fact that if we did not reverse our priorities it would ultimately affect the very fiber of our society, and indeed it has. . . . It's not an

> accident that we have the problems with violence in our communities and the very kind of strange inconsistent moralities that exist today.[10]

Describing its "Program to Disarm Our Communities of Handguns" the national office of the Fellowship of Reconciliation says in its leaflet, "Disarm Locally and Globally,":

> The U.S. is number one in arms exports, possession of nuclear weapons, military strength and handgun deaths. *The use of violence abroad contributes to violence at home* [emphasis added]. The Fellowship of Reconciliation believes that the disarmament agenda for the rest of the decade must address the entire culture of violence — from semi-automatic assault weapons used on our streets, to cruise missiles used to bomb the streets of Third World countries.[11]

Decades ago in the Cold War era, Father Richard McSorley, S.J., asserted that getting rid of societal violence depended on renouncing our willingness to use massive military violence. "The taproot of violence in our society is our intent to use nuclear weapons," he warned. "Once we have agreed to that, all other evil is minor in comparison. Until we squarely face the question of our consent to use nuclear weapons, any hope of large scale improvement of public morality is doomed to failure."

Certainly the willingness to exterminate tens of millions of helpless civilians in a few seconds constitutes today's worst possible violence, but the existence of all other kinds of military weaponry, whether used in actual warfare or in preparation for it, are a major influence in the growing addiction of our society to violence. It is no mere coincidence that the world's militarily most powerful nation also has the most civilian violence.

Father McSorley agrees. In a letter written in 1984 he said: "The Department of Defense still represents the worst violence we have in the country because the extent and the effect of the violence on the people is greater than any other violence. . . . The education for violence continues with the awards we give soldiers, the monuments we erect to past wars. . . . All that says to the citizen and the young man is 'our country approves of killing people.'"

National murder statistics presently number in two years almost as many as the 55,000 U.S. soldiers who died in Vietnam. Homicide is now the tenth leading cause of death in the U.S., a rate many times higher than that of any other western industrialized nation. The high approval rating given President Bush after the Gulf War shows that most citizens support governmental violence, even for such self-interests as oil. Commenting on our endorsement of violence, writer Jim Wallis asks: "Might we better understand our cultural acceptance of violence by looking to the military leaders who casually spoke of 'eliminating the enemy' on video-game-like radar screens or presidents who boasted about 'kicking ass' in Middle East wars?" [12]

Wallis poses a similar question in relation to street crime. In a 1989 *Washington Post* series, "At the Roots of the Violence," a drug dealer, asked why they were always so ready to shoot, said: "I guess it's the greed for that money." Regarding the paper's comment, "It is a way of life that flies in the face of traditional American values," Wallis asks: "Was the reporter right? What have been the values reflected in American foreign policy? What code of ethics governs the wars of Wall Street? How does the enshrinement of violence of greed every day on television sets and movie screens shape our cultural values?" [13]

According to the National Rifle Association, some 200 million firearms are in the hands of private citizens. Most of these, including some three million assault weapons, like the arms of the Pentagon, are carried for defense. Students daily carry an estimated 270 thousand guns to school. Some readers may be unaware of the extent to which our youth are becoming addicted to violence, that every five minutes one is arrested for a violent crime. Marion Wright Edelman, founder and executive director of the Children's Defense Fund, blames militarism for some of it:

> Our kids aren't going to do what we tell them to do, they do what we do. . . . They watch our military expenditures and the way we resolve all of our disputes, and they think that the way that you are powerful and resolve disputes is through more and bigger weapons. They see — whether it's on TV or in all our cultural signals — that what is glamorous and powerful is behind the barrel of a gun.[14]

If children are not literally noticing the dollar signs of our war chests they are very aware of the weaponry itself. How they are conditioned by their culture's addiction to violence has been well studied by the American Psychological Association. Here are some of their findings:

> A plethora of guns and war toys are coveted and possessed by small children. Although few Americans would claim to enjoy or encourage violence, many, at the very minimum, passively condone aggression and violence through acceptance of current film and television productions.

> There is absolutely no doubt that higher levels of viewing violence on television are correlated with increased acceptance of aggressive attitudes and increased aggressive behavior. Three major national studies . . . reviewed hundreds of studies to arrive at the irrefutable conclusion that viewing violence increases violence. In addition, prolonged viewing of media violence can lead to emotional desensitization toward violence.
>
> Desensitization to violence [results] in callused attitudes towards violence directed towards others and a decreased likelihood to take action on behalf of the victim when violence occurs. . . .
>
> Viewing violence increases fear of becoming a victim of violence, with a resultant increase in self-protective behaviors and increased mistrust of others.
>
> Viewing violence *increases viewer's appetites for becoming involved in violence* or exposing themselves to it. [emphasis added][15]

Although this specialized study does not distinguish between fictional and actual violence in the media, it seems safe to assume that prolonged exposure to either leads to similar results, and that action news showing U.S. troops in combat, "smart bombs" blasting buildings, tanks and ships firing big guns, all play some part in seeming to validate and support street violence as a way of meeting problems. That such inevitable news and/or the general public psychology that prevails in wartime directly affects street crime has been documented in research cited by John Swomley:

> A study by Charles Rebber, who has a doctorate in clinical psychology from Rutgers University, demonstrates that combined figures on murder, rape, and aggravated assault in the Uniform Crime Reports rise when the U.S. goes to war. In the wake of the 1983 invasion of Grenada, the figures rose by four percent. After U.S. planes bombed Libya in 1986 the figure rose by thirteen percent. In 1978 after U.S. attacks on Iranian ships the figure rose by five percent, and in 1990 after the invasion of Panama, more people were murdered in the U. S. than in any previous year. Nonviolent crime by contrast showed no similar correlation.[16]

Our Pentagon represents the most powerful potential violence in the world today, and along with TV and movie violence, would seem an important bad influence to be eliminated in any program against street violence. Writer Wendell Berry has pointed out the basic similarity between the government killing people in the Persian Gulf War to satisfy an addiction for oil, and street youth killing for addictions to drugs.[17]

Unfortunately killing itself is now an addiction, occurring whether drugs are involved or not. And just as education in conflict resolution is a better substitute for such violence, so is the nonviolent resistance of civilian-based defense the timely alternative to the "legalized violence" inherent in the Pentagon.

Writer Michael True has noticed the numerical relationship between U.S. violence abroad and at home:

> Understanding ourselves involves recognizing connections between circumstances at home and our behavior abroad. . . . Increasingly, the terror we inflict on others abroad has come home to roost. The United States kills four times as many of its own people per 100,000 as the next most violent nation. And, according to a recent article in the *Wall Street Journal*, we now sell four times as many tanks and warplanes abroad as France, Britain, and Germany combined.
>
> Is the increase in violence at home a direct result of the violence we inflict abroad? I think so.[18]

Although few people might consider the "four times" a coincidence, many might agree with his conclusion. As a religious person, I very much agree. I believe in the moral law which says we reap what we sow, that we are as subject to it as we are to the law of gravity, laws of mathematics, etc. Further, as a Christian pacifist, I believe that not only individuals but whole nations are, in some way, under its jurisdiction. We are affirming this for the U.S. each time we say in the pledge of allegiance that we are a "nation under God." As a superpower we may be free to do as we like, but we are not free from the consequences.

Jesus made a specific application of moral law when he said "All they that take the sword shall perish by the sword." In our democracy, where we all bear some responsibility for what the U.S. does, it is not difficult for me to believe that not only our armed personnel who shoot to kill, or our civilians who make bombs, but all of us are the "All they." If the majority in the U.S. acquiesce to military preparations to kill innocent and guilty alike anywhere in the world, then both innocent and guilty may be killed in our own neighborhoods.

Besides whatever responsibility our militarism has for ordinary street crime is its more direct responsibility for lesser political violence here at home. History shows that small and weak but very nationalistic peoples who feel oppressed may resort to terrorism against those they consider responsible. For over a century we have read of bombing attacks on British civilians which are acknowledged by the Irish Republican Army. For decades, there have been similar acts committed by Palestinians in response to the repression they have experienced under military occupation. In 1993 six U.S. civilians were killed and one thousand injured in Manhattan's World Trade Center by a noontime blast of a 1,200 pound bomb. Sentenced to life were four "Islamic militants" who "sought to punish U.S. for backing Israel." [19] According to the trial judge, who said if the bomb had been placed at the base of the North Tower "as many as ten thousand deaths could have resulted," the defendants showed no remorse, only "arrogance."

One of the four was also convicted for his anonymous letter to the *New York Times* threatening more violence unless the U.S. ended all aid to Israel. In a second trial, the biggest in U.S. history, Sheik Omar Abdul Rahman and nine co-defendants were sentenced to life imprisonment for conspiring to blow up the United Nations and two vehicular tunnels under the Hudson River.

Since the end of the Cold War, our foreign arms sales jeopardizing civilians here at home have reached an average of $17 billion per year. The Congressional Research Service has reported we are the leading supplier to developing countries by a three-to-one margin — sales which are actively promoted by both our Defense and Commerce Departments. Most U.S. citizens are only passively aware of the thousands of civilians in small countries around the world killed each year by U.S.-made guns and bombs, causing intense hatred of this country.

In addition to this international terrorism the U.S. in April 1995 tragically found itself faced with a political form of domestic terrorism. Many of us learned for the first time the extent of the growth of the private militia movement. Just weeks before the shattering blast of the Federal Building in Oklahoma City, the newsletter of the Civilian-Based Defense Association (Omaha) featured articles about the little-known movement. The lead piece by Mel Beckman pointed out that were the U.S. to have civilians trained in unarmed defense the militias would see themselves as unneeded. Millions of nonviolent resisters would already be assuring protection against coups or a feared government itself. In another chapter I show how attempted takeovers in both the Philippines and Russia were defeated by unarmed citizens using nonviolent tactics.

What I have said about the influence of the Pentagon on the ongoing nonpolitical violence of the street — unintentionally validating violence as the ultimate force — would similarly apply to militias. In the newsletter mentioned John Trochmann, a militia promoter, is quoted as saying, "We want to use the ballot box and the jury box. We don't want to go to the cartridge box. But we will if we have to."

Lastly, military establishments with their centralized control have traditionally been tempting targets to seize by rightists and leftists alike. But a U.S. which had — instead of a Pentagon — some tens of millions of decentralized civilians trained in nonviolent defense would offer no such opportunity.

Although the Soviet "threat" is gone, military actions such as those in Grenada, Panama, Somalia, Iraq, Haiti, and Bosnia are slated to continue. The DOD now plans to act as a Department of Intervention, free to go into any country whose economic policies offend our business interests. Warning of "new dangers," it says we as the world's only superpower must be able to wage two wars simultaneously with no help. The 296,000 troops it had abroad in 1992 will be reduced, but the plan still leaves 100,000 in 1996 in Europe alone. The Clinton administration–DOD estimates for the military budget in 1999 is $232 billion, only slightly less than the average at the height of the Cold War; for 1948–1989 — excluding hot war spending for Korea and Vietnam — this annual spending in constant dollars was $250 billion.[20] The 1994 Congress declared there would be no tax-cutting for defense but advocated an increase in the Pentagon budget. There should be no expectation that we need only wait for the debilitating situation to improve — that time alone heals all. The U.S. arms industry hopes to continue to make huge profits at taxpayers' expense and from arms sales abroad.

So far the urgent reasons for getting rid of our present military "defense" program have been in the practical, self-interest of the U.S. — jobs, the economy, street violence, ecology. For pacifists like myself there is a far greater additional reason: any shooting war is morally wrong. The actual carnage may be far away, as in both World Wars, Korea, Vietnam, and Iraq, and most of us, along with our families, and our cities, may be safe on our own soil, but "legalized murder" of human beings anywhere is wrong. And for pacifists, preparing for it is also wrong. I consider our readiness and willingness "when necessary" to kill tens of thousands with conventional weapons, or tens of millions with nuclear weapons, a supreme evil.

Pacifists and other idealists can hope that when global disputes arise in the distant future, a more intelligent way than warfare will become universally recognized as standard procedure. In our own country, after the Civil War no state armed itself against another. One day nations may do likewise, and rely on some sort of World Court in case of disputes. They will see that warfare is not only too obscene but that for every victor there is a loser. Until that enlightened day, civilian-based nonviolent defense seems the best way to defend the U.S. from some as-yet-unknown aggressive superpower. The price we are paying presently in higher taxes, higher costs of living, unemployment, poor education and health services, degradation of the environment, and some part of street crime, must not continue.

2

Terminologies; Martin Luther King, Jr.'s Six Characteristics of Nonviolent Action

In this chapter we will examine some of the terminology of the alternatives to military defense. The most inclusive term, "civilian-based defense," covers all types of opposition by unarmed civilians to an aggressor. In Europe the term is often shortened to "civilian defense" which should not be confused with wartime "civil defense." In South Africa Gandhi offered a prize for a substitute for the then-common term "passive resistance" and adopted the coinage *satyagraha*. Literally this means "holding to the truth," or standing fast with truth, his favorite synonym for a loving God.

The preferred English equivalent has been "nonviolence." Sometimes such negative terms are very specific such as in the word "nonsense." In other cases defining something by what it is not can be overly broad. A cup of water may be harmless, but to say it represents "nonviolence" is meaningless. Only occasionally did Gandhi use the Hindi equivalent *ahimsa*. Today "nonviolence" is widely used to cover actions better described as "unviolent." Settling a dispute in court is not violence, but it is more the way of ahimsa than satyagraha. The latter is needed when there is no *un*violent solution.

One writer has used the term "transforming power of spirit" which is unwieldy but might be a more accurate description. Eliminating an enemy by transforming her/him into a friend instead of into a corpse is basic to satyagraha. King, in his *Stride Towards Freedom,* places this characteristic high on his list of six:

> First . . . nonviolent resistance is not a method for cowards; it does resist. If one uses this method because he (she) is afraid or merely because he (she) lacks the instruments of violence, he (she) is not truly nonviolent.
>
> A second basic fact that characterizes nonviolence is that it does not seek to defeat or humiliate an opponent but to win his (her) friendship.
>
> A third characteristic . . . is that the attack is directed against the forces of evil rather than against persons who happen to be doing the evil.
>
> A fourth point . . . is a willingness to accept suffering without retaliation, to accept blows without striking back. [This is perhaps nonviolence/satyagraha's most unique characteristic.]
>
> A fifth point concerning nonviolent resistance is that it avoids not only external violence but also internal violence of the spirit. The nonviolent resister not only refuses to shoot (an) opponent but also to hate him (her).
>
> A sixth basic fact . . . is that it is based on the conviction that the universe is on the side of justice . . . the believer in nonviolence has a deep faith in the future.[1]

Interestingly, King does not discuss here Gandhi's favorite term, "Truth." In most nonviolent actions, honesty has a high priority, but in special situations, such as saving the lives of Jews in World War II, or sabotaging property, deception is often required. Whether such duplicities may properly be included in definitions of "nonviolent action" is an open question. After having previously openly engaged in it, Gandhi himself considered property destruction a "form of violence." The government of South Africa called the African National Congress a violent organization because, although it tended not to attack people, it did engage in property destruction. On the other hand, some of the best known and respected nonviolent activists have declared responsibility for weapons destruction and have gone to prison.

King's first point, "it does resist," seems on the surface the opposite of Jesus' "Do not resist one who is evil." But Walter Wink has shown that the translation "resist" derives from *anthistemi*, (Greek) which means a violent form of reaction. Wink says: "A proper translation of Jesus' admonition would then be, 'Do not strike back at evil (or, one who has done you evil) in kind. Do not give blow for blow. Do not retaliate against violence with violence.' Jesus was no less committed to opposing evil than the anti-Roman resistance fighters. The only difference was over the means to be used: *how* one should fight evil." [2] Wink points out that carrying a soldier's pack more than one mile was a violation of military law, and could put the soldier in jeopardy. Today's nonviolent resister would probably practice "civil disobedience" by refusing to walk even the first mile for the oppressor, and go to jail.

3

Bertrand Russell's Civilian Defense Proposals; Jessie Wallace Hughan

In World War I the British philosopher Bertrand Russell, then a pacifist, proposed that his country totally disarm and defend itself by civilian resistance:

> Let us imagine that England were to disband its army and navy after a generation of instruction in the principles of passive resistance as a better defense than war. Let us suppose that England at the same time publicly announced that no armed opposition would be offered to an invader, that all might come freely, but that no obedience would be yielded to any commands that a foreign authority might issue. What would happen in this case?[1]

Russell answered by imagining that the German government might try to take advantage of Britain's military helplessness. Most Germans would then oppose the venture, for they could not be given the usual pretext of "defense" of Germany, or of some other nations, for such an invasion. But, he suggested:

> . . . Let us suppose all home opposition [is] overcome, and a force [is] dispatched to England to take possession of the country. Such a force . . . would not be in the state of mingled fear and ferocity which characterizes an invading army among a hostile population. There would be no difficulty in preserving discipline, and no

opportunity for the rape and rapine which have always been displayed by troops after victory in battle.

Russell then pictured the Germans setting up their own government in London with some of their own administrators and issuing edicts:

> But at this point, if the nation showed as much courage as it always has shown in fighting, difficulties would begin. All the existing officials would refuse to cooperate with the Germans. Some of the more prominent would be imprisoned, perhaps even shot. . . . But if the others held firm, if they continued to carry out the decrees previously made by the English Parliament and the English Government, the Germans would have to dismiss them all, even to the humblest post, and call in German talent to fill the breach.
>
> And it would be very difficult for the Germans suddenly, out of nothing, to create an administrative machine. Whatever edicts they might issue would be quietly ignored by the population. If they ordered that German should be the language taught in schools, the schoolmasters would go on as if no such order had been issued; if the schoolmasters were dismissed, the parents would no longer send the children to school.

(Russell here was prophetic about the nonviolent resistance of Norwegian teachers and parents against Nazis in World War II a quarter of a century later.)

> If they tried to take over the railways, there would be a strike of the railway servants. Whatever they touched would instantly become paralyzed, and it would soon be evident . . . that nothing was to be made out of England. . . .

At the outset of World War II the pacifist Jessie Hughan, saying nothing had occurred since Russell's proposal to destroy its validity, proposed the same defense for the United States:

> First, [the disarmed nation] would rid itself of the few incentives it still holds forth to international robbery.
>
> Second, it would put in practice, with the aid of organized international machinery, such enlightened foreign policies as to bind all other nations to itself with ties of friendship and mutual interest.
>
> Third, by frank gesture of complete and open disarmament it would destroy all fear and distrust of itself in the minds of its neighbors.
>
> Fourth, it would bring home to its people through practical experience the value of liberty and democracy as to lead the average

> citizen to choose hardship, imprisonment, and even death rather than to submit to dictatorship, foreign or domestic.
>
> Fifth, it would prepare a deliberate system of nonviolent defense . . . with the purpose of preventing any potential aggressor, however ruthless, from achieving the objectives for which the invasion might be undertaken.[2]

Hughan's "deliberate system" had four points:

1. No services or supplies to be furnished to invaders.
2. No orders to be obeyed except those of the constitutional government.
3. No insult or injury to be offered the invaders.
4. All public officials to be pledged to die rather than surrender.

Her fourth requirement seems an unnecessary impediment to the adoption of this type of national defense. City officials should be elected on their competency, not on willingness to be martyred. Should any invader be so crude as to threaten executions for refusal to sign surrender terms, the entire nation— the whole world — could declare any contract signed under duress as null and void.

After Russell's and Hughan's proposals, India finally freed itself from the occupying British, making use of the methods suggested, and other subject nations have successfully used similar tactics. In some, good examples of satyagraha were mixed in with outright violence. These cases are examined in a later chapter. Concurrent with some modern events have been writings on civilian-based defense by several others, both here and abroad. Most extensive are the works of Gene Sharp, whose prize-winning essay "Making the Abolition of War a Realistic Goal," would serve as valuable introductory material to this book.

Among his important points is that no nation is going to "choose to be defenseless." We in the peace movement, like Russell, Hughan, and others must offer some alternative for a Pentagon. We must remember that the power of an invader does not lie in his capacity for violence but rather in the "obedience, submission, and cooperation" of the invaded.

Napoleon, at the height of his success, reflected that: "There are only two forces in the world: the spirit and the sword. And the spirit always conquers the sword." The spirit of an invaded people who know that they, not the invader, have the ultimate power, could be very high.

4

Scenario: Superpower Axis X Invades Disarmed U.S.

Here is a future scenario we might consider. Let us assume that around 2000 A.D. the world's military leaders agree that nuclear weapons no longer serve any purpose and, under United Nations supervision, should be abolished. All nuclear powers are glad to get rid of the liability and to rely entirely on conventional armament. The world is relieved that the possibility of hundreds of millions of helpless people dying from the blast, heat, and radiation of a deliberate or accidental nuclear war is gone at last.

Yet, alas, all realize that any former nuclear power, faced with losing a conventional war, might resort to making such weapons again rather than suffer defeat. The only logical solution, as Jonathan Schell and others pointed out long ago, is to be rid of conventional armaments, too. World economists, bankers, industrialists, agriculturists, and others advise that getting rid of the crushing burden of conventional armaments (nuclear arms represent a small percentage) is key to solving the world's massive indebtedness. It is also key to eliminating mass starvation and homelessness, with their potential for violent revolutions. But no universal agreement could be reached for abolishing all conventional weapons.[1]

At this point, in the year 2005, the United States, with the highest military budget of any nation and with the most to gain economically, makes a drastic proposal: It invites all others to follow its lead in a world disarmament race. It will unilaterally disarm itself twenty percent each year as an example for other nations to emulate. Without waiting for others to do likewise, it will continue until, at the end of five years, it will be totally free of all kinds of military weapons and armed forces.

The U.S. can risk this because its citizens voted to defend themselves entirely by non-military means. Because the programs of Gandhi and King were so successful, the U.S. will adopt the form of nonviolent resistance exemplified by them. Its citizens will train themselves to resist any invasion. They no longer want to waste hundreds of billions in taxes each year on the Pentagon and on interest payments on the two-thirds of the national debt it is responsible for.

As a beginning the government announces a contest to seek a better term than either satyagraha or "nonviolence," and it adopts the acronym ANAVET: "Action Negating All Violence and Establishing Trust" — which covers King's first five points. Negating violence means not only that defenders refuse to use violence but also that they refuse to accept or be intimidated by violence or any threat of it. Thus, should a bayoneter order "Move!", the resister trained in ANAVET remains as stationary as possible. His/her body may writhe in pain if cut, or fall to the ground if jabbed, but the intent of the violence-backed order is "negated." The resister might sing "We shall not be moved," but eye contact, however serious, remains friendly, and never expresses hatred. The second half of ANAVET excludes most forms of deception, and sabotage involving secrecy. The government decides that establishing trust with invaders is more important for defense than physical advantage gained by undercover destruction of weaponry.

Suppose that in 2010 the United States detonates on schedule its very last bomb. At the same ceremony the Secretary of ANAVET National Defense announces the list of nations joining this phased annual reduction of conventional weapons. It is hoped that the entire world will soon join this last step and become totally disarmed.

Along with this the United States shifts from a wasteful wartime economy to a productive peacetime one. Once again made-in-the-USA products sell competitively in world markets, even alongside those of the two presently disarmed nations, Japan and Germany. Free of debt and able to negotiate attractive financial agreements with other nations, the U.S. makes friends abroad without making enemies and gains the respect and admiration of the international community.

For me, and perhaps for most readers, this book logically should end at this point. No nation would have a reason to invade the United States. There would no longer be overseas bases for big nations to fear, no gunboat diplomacy for small nations to resent. But what about greed, the other reason for invasions mentioned by Hughan, such as was evident in the occupation of Kuwait by Iraq in 1990? She specifies ridding an unarmed country of "incentives" for international robbery which are usually justified by some sort of historical claim.

There could be many such possible claims against the United States. Mexico might claim the entire Southwest, saying it was seized as spoils of the Mexican War. Russia might claim it was cheated out of Alaska, only fifteen miles across the Bering Sea. Native American nations within the United States could all claim their vast territories. Nicaragua might claim the millions in damages it was awarded by the World Court for the mining of its harbor by the CIA, a judgment ignored by the United States.

Claims have resulted in invasions. Hitler's 1939 invasion of Poland began with Germany's justifiable claim that Poland was holding Danzig in defiance of a League of Nations order to return it. Iraq had long claimed that it and Kuwait were part of the same nation until separated by British imperialism. To this it added a later grievance that Kuwait pumped more oil from their common under-the-border pool than the rules permitted. But however valid the foregoing claims, the world has rightly condemned both Hitler and Hussein for their brutal aggressions.

An unarmed United States, in its new debt-free prosperity, could well afford to make some amends to those it had exploited. With perhaps a million new jobs it might welcome new resident workers from Mexico. Native Americans might find their unfriendly homelands made more productive; some of the nearly half of all technologists in the United States presently employed in the non-productive "defense" industry might discover more economic methods of converting sea water to fresh, opening vast deserts to rich farmland. Awards for valid claims would be made from strength, not weakness. If negotiations broke off because the demands were excessive and the other side threatened invasion, the United States would resist with ANAVET.

The process might be likened to modern labor-management disputes. When long and serious negotiations end without agreement, a union calls a strike, a form of nonviolent non-cooperation. Management may sit it out, shut down, hire scabs, etc. but there need be no exacerbating violence. There are those of us who recall former days when most strike news was about violence — police and national guard killing strikers and strikers bombing factories. As late as 1937, on the same afternoon I drove through the city, thirteen steelworkers were killed in a strike demonstration in Gary, Indiana.

Ideally, people should always be able to "sit down and talk it out," but experience says otherwise. Both management and labor may have the common goal of a company making more money and satisfactorily dividing it, but walkouts continue. Today if labor-management negotiations prove futile, courts, not violence, are the expected last resort. Nations, however, still insist on their sovereignty and prefer international anarchy to the World Court or resolutions of the United Nations, and when negotiations break off, they rely on armaments as a last resort. As von Clausewitz said, they "continue" their diplomacy in warfare.

I cannot envision any credible reason that an unarmed, unfeared, and respected United States, as the one just described, would ever be attacked. But because most people, as Gene Sharp says, need some assurance they are not defenseless, we shall contrive a necessarily unbelievable scenario to illustrate in detail how those same people, without any of the usual weaponry, could repel a mighty invasion. To suggest a very broad illustration, one setting will be metropolitan New York City and the other rural Virginia.

Scenario: Suppose that in 2010 some nations in an alliance of superpowers called Axis X are suspicious of the claim of the United States that it is now unarmed. The Axis insists the UN Disarmament Verification Commission order the vault in Fort Knox, Kentucky, be opened for inspection. The U.S. maintains that its "Bullion Depository," according to long-standing security policy, has never been open to anyone except designated personnel. The UN Assembly concurs, saying aerial reconnaissance has shown no possible transfer into the vault of anything but gold bars.

Axis X then asks if the UN has also monitored all shipments *out* of Knox, such as to the Treasury Department's New York Assay Office. The UN says no, it has never examined shipments from Knox, nor shipments from the Assay Office in Lower Manhattan to the nearby Federal Reserve Bank of New York in the Financial District. The Axis leaders then insist Fort Knox and all Manhattan vaults where any gold bars are deposited be inspected. When the UN begins debating this demand the Axis objects that this is allowing time for tritium to be removed, and that if there is no inspection within ten days the vaults will be forcibly opened by its military forces.

The United States, which says it will not open any vaults except by vote of the UN and feels itself fully as independently strong when armed nonviolently as when armed violently, refuses any compliance with the military threat. The Axis nations, like most, want to project a favorable image. Thus, when announcing the "intervention to assist the United Nations," they say it is to expose probable sources of tritium which could be used in missiles secretly deployed elsewhere, claiming that these are "military operations done in the interests of world peace." We may assume the Axis needs world trade for its full economic life, profitably selling surpluses and importing items in short supply. For some minerals it may be totally dependent on outside sources. Many people around the world will believe this — certainly most inside Axis X itself. In our scenario, among the few inside Axis X who do not believe the claim are some of its top leaders who are more interested in robbing the vaults of gold for the Axis' failing, militarily burdened economy than in uncovering tritium.

If the reader is not merely amused by this contrived plot, s/he is invited to invent another. As stated, this writer believes a well-respected United States, freed from the crushing burden of armaments and free to help other nations without invading them, would itself never be invaded. Even accepting the scenario's original demand, certainly the UN and the United States, given time, could negotiate an inspection of always-secret Fort Knox. In fact, we may suppose such a way is found but ignored by Axis X, a clear indication of the real purpose of the invasion. In this scenario, saving the treasure of Fort Knox will be the final responsibility of an unarmed defense which is facing a mighty Axis X with an enormous army, navy, and air force, as well as ample tanks, missiles, artillery, battleships, cruisers, submarines, carriers, bombers and fighters.

The UN and most of its member nations individually, including close allies of Axis X, would denounce the pretext for invading a friendly and non-threatening United States. As soon as troopships were on course for New York, the city would prepare for the probable invasion. The existing "peacetime" number of its trained ANAVET defenders might be only one hundred thousand women and men — many more would need to be hastily added. Of Manhattan's total population, perhaps half would need evacuation and temporary housing. First of these would be hospital patients, jail inmates and institutionalized others. Next would come most children under high school age, and then those elderly and disabled who would have the most difficulty without electricity — especially those living on upper floors — should utility shutoffs be necessary. Continuous broadcasts would announce that as far as possible gas and electricity would be selectively turned off only in areas actually invaded. Water would retain a minimum flow, but without electricity it would reach only to about fifth floors in most of Manhattan.

By the time world satellite news predicted that four troopships were two days from docking, every operable vehicle on Manhattan's streets and every subway would be entering the borough near its lower, southern end and would be running mostly one-way uptown to the north to pick up waiting evacuees with hand luggage. These would then be

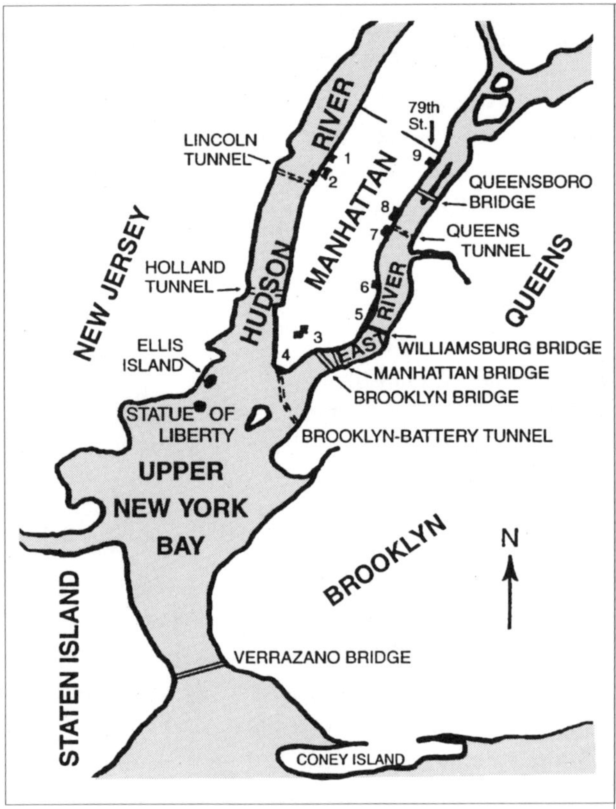

Figure B. Map of New York Harbor and Manhattan Island.

Key:

1. Powerplant, "59th Street," seized by paratroopers.
2. Passenger Ship Terminal, Piers 88–92 (left); DeWitt Clinton Park (right), first troop encampment.
3. City Hall and Park and Municipal Building, third encampment.
4. Battery Park, second encampment.
5. East River Park, fourth encampment.
6. "East River" Powerplant, seized by paratroopers.
7. "Waterside" Powerplant, seized by paratroopers.
8. United Nations.
9. Powerplant, "79th Street," seized by paratroopers.

deposited at improvised transfer points in neighboring Bronx, Queens, and New Jersey for longer trips to temporary housing outside the area.

Ideally all citizens of a disarmed United States would be trained as active defenders, but such seems far from necessary. It is estimated that in the whole of India fewer than 400,000 were trained in satyagraha; another estimate is less than two million. Besides Manhattan's core of 100,000 already trained would be others remaining in town to enlist in ANAVET practice sessions. The largest group of residents staying would consist of many who, while unwilling to risk confrontational dangers, might be willing to be passive residents, planning to move later if life under an attempted occupation became too rough. More than enough Manhattanites would stay for the city to be almost fully functioning after evacuation.

Meanwhile from Washington D.C. the battle for world support would be in full force. Around the globe people would see news photos and video footage of evacuees and the approaching troopships. They would repeatedly hear that the United States was totally disarmed and that its only defense would be ANAVET. From Axis X they would continue to hear that this was a pretext to hide tritium, and on TV they would watch bomb shelter drills in Axis X. Troops aboard huge transport liners would be told that they were heroes risking their lives to expose secret weaponry which might obliterate them at any moment.

Before any soldiers sighted land, commando-type paratroopers of Axis X would make a surprise drop on Manhattan power plants. The city made no secret that when it turned off its electricity the borough would be all but useless. (An example: gas station pumps operate electrically; street vehicles would stop when out of fuel.)

A commando paratrooper assigned a key secret mission might be the most difficult of all soldiers with whom to "negate all violence." Desperate, fearful, and racing against time, he has been conditioned to obliterate any interference, to kill with little provocation. An ANAVET resister, facing the commando's automatic rifle and refusing the order to "Stand aside" could well expect to be blasted. But the well-planned defense of Manhattan would allow a compromise here by making the order and the blocking unimportant. An air strike to occupy such strategic points would have been anticipated.

Advance arrangements would have been made to evacuate operating personnel and to switch plants to outside computer control, to take them off-line and to shut them down. Street resisters would merely remind the few dozen commandos — who presumably understand English — that they were invading an unarmed country.

Manhattan plants burn mostly gas which is easily turned off, and some oil. Enough of the latter would be kept on hand to run ten days independently of outside supply. This reserve would be appropriately reduced at the first indication of a possible invasion. The balance of oil would start to be used up as soon as troopships were on course for New York. Any left when the parachutists were descending would have to be hastily dumped into the Hudson and/or East River — much to the horror of environmentalists watching on TV! Steam would thin the heavy black oil for faster dumping. A trained chutist coming down on a power plant and seeing vaporous clouds at its dock, and a containing boom being towed into place around an oil slick, would know some fuel was on hand. Steam vented from chimneys would mean the tank was empty.

There might be dummy plant personnel, ANAVET volunteers, occupying the places of the absent experienced operators. When chutists would occupy such a plant and demand its continued operation, the replacements could explain that their job was to remove name plates and other identification from control panels, that they knew nothing about running the plant which was now being shut down by outside control. Boilers would gradually cool and turbines spin to a stop, and all electricity for Manhattan would come from a nationwide emergency grid, later turned off selectively in any area invaded. If Axis X wanted Manhattan plants operating it would have to bring in its own operators and fuel, all tankers with oil having left the harbor.

In the best case, there would need to be emergency oil dumping at only one or two plants. An ANAVET resister instructed in dumping, or a regular dock employee who is also a trained resister, could oversee the steam and oil coming from an open pipe close to the river surface. By letting the water flow into the tank, the oil above it would be displaced and no pumping power would be needed. This worker, when questioned by captors, might correctly answer that the operation was entirely under remote computer control. But they might assume, also correctly, that this worker could order the dumping to stop. They might produce a portable phone and demand compliance.

This person on an oil tanker dock might well be the first resister of the invasion to be physically abused. Depending on how rushed they felt, chutists on the dock might do any beating or jabbing under cover rather than on the open platform where it might be photographed by helicopters of a UN inspection team and the news media. As for being threatened with death, the captive would know he/she was too important to be killed. Threats against the captive's family also would have little weight, all computerized files with home addresses having been removed from plant offices.

In the UN the paratroop drop would be ample reason for the U.S. ambassador to call for a world boycott of Axis X for its naked armed aggression. Ongoing General Assembly sessions would soon hear that four of the world's largest ocean liners, the former *Queen Elizabeth II (QE2)*, *Oriana*, *Michelangelo*, and *France*, now operated by Axis X and crammed with soldiers, were nearing Coney Island. TV news would show the ocean filled with thousands of small boats with ANAVET crews.

When lead-ship *QE2* entered the channel it would be surrounded by inflatable rafts, dinghies, and expendable rowboats, the flotilla's smallest craft, which would be maneuvering directly into the slow-moving liner's path. When about to be rammed, their crews would jump overboard. Larger powerboats and sailboats, adjacent but not close enough to be rammed, would expect to be hit with firehose jets and possibly upset. Those farther away could be overturned by the wash of the ships' several escorting helicopters. Sails might be quickly dropped whenever a helicopter approached, then raised again. Farthest away would be larger yachts and commercial fishing boats. The Department of ANAVET National Defense would compensate all volunteers and boat owners for operating expenses and for injuries to life and property.

The main purpose of such a symbolic blockade would be to inform as directly as possible all *QE2* officers, soldiers and sailors that, contrary to Axis X briefings and broadcasts, they had not been invited by the UN to search Manhattan vaults for tritium. On the contrary, the UN had condemned the invasion. Banners on power boats and signs on sails might read:

UN SAYS NO TRITIUM HERE

U.S. TOTALLY UNARMED

UN CONDEMNS YOUR AGGRESSION

All this would be in the language(s) of Axis X, as would be similar messages from flotilla public address horns and the thousands of leaflets which would be dropped from planes high above Axis X's helicopters.

Below the leafleting planes would be helicopters with neutral UN observers and news reporters transmitting live reports via satellite.

Above all of these would be reconnaissance satellites of the UN Disarmament Verification Commission and of individual nations, including the United States. In the eighties, spy satellites could read license plates of street vehicles and see through clouds and in the dark. Perhaps in 2010 they will identify upturned faces of swimmers from overturned boats! We might assume that Axis X in 2011 would be able to shoot down most or even all U.S. satellites. If so, it would probably be very careful not to damage any such belonging to other nations or to the UN. As this is written no known anti-satellite weaponry actually exists, and the U.S. so far is resisting such development lest it start a space arms race.

World viewers of such physically weak and vulnerable protests could be profoundly affected. After the determined symbolic blockade in New Zealand, American Ambassador Anne Martindell, urging no more warships be sent to that nation, testified before Congress in 1985: "I have not been able to put out of my mind the frightening picture of a young woman protester in a rowboat, holding a baby in her arms, with the slowly moving submarine bearing down on it and barely missing running over it."

Army troops, aware or not of worldwide coverage, would be confined below deck to shield them from all leaflets, posters, banners, and PA horns (they would be told it was for protection against enemy snipers.) Only sailors not expected to land would be allowed above deck to trash leaflets and send water jets against flotilla craft. But on jammed troopships carrying several times their normal number of passengers, it would be difficult to prevent the grapevine from circulating more information below decks than might be seen through broken plastic covers of portholes.

If the essence of armed conflict is to win the opponent's territory, the essence of satyagraha is to win the opponent's mind. How and what is said on leaflets would be of first importance. Next would come methods of distribution, and perhaps a new kind of leaflet. Former weapons designers might have invented a sticky, double-faced leaflet, whose second side, no matter how it landed, would stick to the surface and its top side could he read. Not sticking together, they could be bundled, etc. To minimize being shot down, leafleting planes might fly many miles away from the ships, releasing tied bundles whose parachutes would open to allow the bundles to drift into scattering position — all under computer control responding to meteorological conditions. Care would be taken that nothing heavy might fall on targets and cause injuries. If plane casualties warranted, drones could be used, but ruled out would be anything resembling a weapon.

A more personal and concentrated leafleting greeting would occur at the high Verrazano Bridge under which all troopships would pass. From its walkways thousands of ANAVET volunteers would drop more leaflets and hang banners hundreds of feet long. Ship helicopters preceding the leading *QE2* might blast the banners with incendiaries and strafe the walkways. Axis X would claim the leaflet bundles looked like bombs, an allegation disputed by news pictures. Live news showing say ten killed outright and fifty wounded would shock the world. The UN's call for an investigation would be quickly followed by a second and more urgent demand for sanctions.

As the ships approached docking facilities the usual needed assistance would be absent. Manhattan's Passenger Ship Terminal, Piers 88, 90, 92, at the Hudson River foot of 48th to 52nd Streets, is the only dock big enough and deep enough to handle the world's largest ships. Normal docking of a superliner is in the charge of a New York Port Authority harbor pilot, who boards outside the harbor. But now the traditional Pilot Ship would be deserted, providing no expert familiar with the forces of tides, river currents and, especially important to large liners, of wind. The *QE2* towers thirteen stories above water.

The Port Authority would have ended all tug service needed to dock such ships. Finding tugs might be the next task of the ship's helicopters after blasting the bridge, Axis X's own tugs being too slow to accompany the world's fastest liners from home ports. Pre-invasion pictures by the invader's own satellites would have shown that most tugs were dispersing beyond helicopter reach. The few found and boarded by replacement crews would have been rendered inoperable by removal of diesel fuel injection parts. With no tugs or pilots, the ships would have liked to "parallel park" along the half-mile Hudson esplanade of Battery Park City, upstream from the park itself and fronting the familiar World Trade Center towers.

But all such deep-enough waterfronts by now would be blockaded by already-docked freighters, tankers, and barges linked together. All would be crammed with ANAVET resisters and their huge signs. On the East River the blockade would not extend upstream from Brooklyn Bridge, itself a blockade to big liners. (The superstructure of the *QE2* looms forty-five feet above the bridge's mean high water clearance.) Let us assume that therefore the captains agree to continue up the Hudson to the regular Passenger Ship Terminal piers, from which embarking troops could quickly take up positions across the two-mile width of Manhattan to cut it in two. From there the troops would take occupational control of all of Lower Manhattan up to 79th Street — running through Central Park and including the already-captured 79th Street power plant. To allow maneuvering space for unassisted docking, the *QE2* would go first, others awaiting their turn downstream, mid-river between Battery Park on Manhattan's lower tip and Ellis Island. The small-boat flotilla, which would have been keeping up, would now divide, some staying to surround the three waiting.

Before approaching the Terminal the *QE2*'s captain would have decided that blasting the blockading ships out of the way was impractical — sunken wreckage in water just deep enough for his own ship would still prevent reaching the piers. He might correctly assume that, as with the tugs, the ships were not only crewless but inoperable. He would probably decide to board the blockade, untie it from the piers, and let it drift out of the way with the current — now downstream with the outgoing tide. Pointing the *QE2* from directly upstream to slightly towards the blockade, he would let the current push his angled ship alongside the one tanker, three freighters, and a barge. As the towering hull approached, the deck officer would order the bag-like rope fenders lowered.

From the decks of the blockade between the *QE2* and the bulkheads of Piers 88 and 90, resisters would hold their signs facing upwards. Banners would be laid flat on deck. Thousands of troops, earlier kept under cover but now preparing to board, would get a close-up view of "enemy propaganda," updated to include late-breaking news:

INVADERS MASSACRE TEN CIVILIANS ON BRIDGE

UN VOTES SANCTIONS AGAINST AXIS X

There would also be messages relevant to the impending person-to-person confrontation:

ALL U.S. DISARMED

REFUSE ORDERS TO HARM THE HARMLESS

Powerful shore-based PA systems would relay similar messages, and for troops below deck, repeat earlier ones:

U.S. TOTALLY DISARMED

UN SAYS NO TRITIUM

AXIS X GO HOME

By now, if not before, the general in charge of army boarding parties would know he faced a worldwide public relations problem. Telephoto pictures from news helicopters would soon show the one-sided confrontation. Were all news helicopters and even the few from the UN shot down, there would still be satellites. The general might remember that back in the days of President Eisenhower the U2 spy plane could see a golf ball from eighty thousand feet. The *QE2* might lay an old-fashioned smoke screen which would be effective against commercial cameras, but not against satellites seeing through ordinary clouds. Were it available in 2010 he might use some kind of floating cloud of tiny metallized balloons — miniature versions of today's familiar shiny, helium-filled toy balloons.

Looking up from the decks of the three freighters, tanker and barge, resisters would see several gangways swinging out from cargo doors in the hull of the *QE2*, their ends lowering slowly to just over their own heads, none of which would have any kind of helmet. ANAVET volunteers would have spent much time in training sessions discussing the pros and cons of protective gear. Let us assume they decided to wear only normal street clothing appropriate for prevailing weather. There could be several reasons for choosing such physical vulnerability.

First, it assumes the average group of opponents are decent persons. Facing a soldier and wearing a helmet says in effect the resister anticipates being struck, but being completely vulnerable says the resister assumes the soldier to be a human being who is unwilling to injure a defenseless individual. The resister's attire partly sets the tone of the confrontation, and indicates the expectation of whether it will be violent or unviolent. Protective gear makes it easier for soldiers to use the violence they have been trained to use. Street attire tends to give a soldier more of a normal, peacetime mindset, less one of a trained killer on a battlefield.

ANAVET volunteers would also know that just as there are occasional brutes who beat defenseless wives and abuse helpless children, so there may be some soldiers who might enjoy killing unarmed resisters.

Second, choosing vulnerability makes the facial expressions of resisters fully visible. Ideally, faces would show no hostility or fear, yet not appear stoically unconcerned when pain was felt; they would be smiling or serious as called for in the second-by-second situation. Facial visibility would be an important reason not to use gas masks.

Finally, in military offense, an increase in a defender's strength axiomatically calls for increasing offensive strength. Thus helmets which render truncheons less effective would probably result in escalating to water jets, tear gas, etc.

Resisters would now be clustering under the overhead ends of gangways and at the soldiers' two objectives: the cleats with hawsers tying blockading crafts together, and those tying the crafts to piers. Soldiers with truncheons would begin stepping down the steep gangways. Since all would be pushed from behind amidst sharp orders from sergeants, there would be no choice at the bottom but to step off or jump off onto heads below. Many resisters would fall under the weight, as might some soldiers.

All resisters aboard would have been divided into affinity groups of perhaps a dozen and a half, each with its monitor. Normally these groups would make their own consensus decisions about their moves, such as whether to advance or retreat. In training sessions resisters might have practiced blockading soldiers only standing face-to-face. If so, in this unexpected jumping-down tactic they would then rely on instructions from their monitor. By previous agreement, any resister disagreeing with the monitor's decision would be free to question it or, time not permitting, to leave the group.

In any case, the several monitors' responsibility would change from helping the group to blockade, to rescuing individuals who might get trampled. In this sort of football scene resisters would be pulling out the fallen — being as careful with soldiers as with civilians — and helping them to one side. From *QE2* horns would come the loud, repeated, clear order for all civilians to please leave boats and barges and move onto piers, saying that no one complying will be injured in any way. Already photographers in nearby buildings and below any screening clouds would be getting shots of resisters being roughly jumped on.

The rough tactic, however, would gain the soldiers only a limited landing spot, for resisters just a few feet away would still face the butt end of advancing truncheons and impede progress. "Negating" the threatening violence, moving aside only to let trampled victims through, they would stand firm. The bodily push of soldiers would be against packed rows of resisters. But the pressure of butt ends would increase, giving way to short jabs. More wincing resisters would have to retreat, limping through their own lines, or be borne on stretchers to piers. Unlike the 1919 British massacre in Amritsar, where the deaths of 379 unarmed Indians took weeks to become known to the outside world, New York casualties would be seen instantly on international TV.

Those interviewed might mention the old slogan of Gandhi and King campaigns: We will outmatch their ability to inflict suffering with our ability to take it.

For many soldiers, their initial reaction to the struggle, whether looking down from gangways or being in it, might be a feeling of relief that it all was so easy and free of danger. Contrary to days of briefings at sea about terrorist attacks and rushing to subways when the secret missiles came, this first battle would look surprisingly safe! But already word would be passed along that it might be a trap. Ship helicopters scrutinizing pier buildings and higher ones ashore would lend credence to the warning. Aboard, both before and during the first propaganda barrage at sea of signs, leaflets, and PA horns, soldiers had been reminded that enemy claims of disarmament were lies.

Months earlier, when ANAVET training sessions were on world TV and the United States was urging all nations to follow its example, Axis X citizens would have been warned this was a trick to disarm nations so the U.S. with its missiles could subjugate them. Now, some soldiers, especially those in the widening arc of frontline truncheon jabbers, would find it harder to discount such claims. The willingness of New Yorkers to be hurt rather than give way would seem very real and would seem actually to be what the enemy was saying via signs, big horns on piers, and now hand horns on decks. The faint beginnings of troop demoralization would begin.

Generals aboard the *QE2* observing the slow progress below might have mixed emotions when hearing the escalation order to "Swing truncheons!" for they had received helicopter reports of cameras in windows, and the firing on one of them, and of reporters ashore interviewing trampled victims. Now there could be bloodshed. As they watched the army's TV closeups of clubs starting to hit heads and shoulders, they would soon notice that only men were being knocked down. Women, if hit at all, were struck lightly. The generals would also have noticed that while both men and women held up arms to ward off blows, none grappled or tried to hold onto truncheons. This compromise would have been a training session decision. (In the salt works invasion of 1930 in India, satyagraha resisters held arms down during *lathi* attacks.)

The overall result of swinging truncheons would be that mostly men were dragged to safety and not readily replaced, so that soldiers increasingly faced those they liked least to strike — women. Partly for this reason, partly because of the bloodier male victims shown on worldwide TV, the generals might want to switch to tear gas, which treats all alike and at a distance. A soldier might be reluctant to poke or club an unarmed woman face-to-face, but would have no hesitation dropping a gas canister on a steel deck or throwing it from a distance. But the decision would probably be against gas because it could leak to below decks and present a lethal hazard also to troops — now already going down to search for crews who could operate the ships. The generals had already ruled out gas in any enclosed space like buildings, subways, rail cars, and now ships. So the slow and brutal advance by clubbing would continue.

The generals might also have been watching for any growing reluctance to hit even the men. The disarmed United States would have claimed that "any normal, average, mature person" would not continue to inflict injuries on another such person whose words and actions remain continuously devoid of hate and violence. If Axis X leaders might ignore or even ridicule suggestions of a morale problem, the generals would not.

As they watched TV close-ups of the clubbing, they would get a report, the metallized cloud hiding satellite viewing, would last only minutes more. Its stocking had not been predicated on the continued resistance encountered. Under orders to enhance the image of Axis X as the great crusader for world peace, the generals would hope to hide sickening scenes. In this unhappy situation they might make a seemingly paradoxical decision: They would switch to bayonets to speed up deck clearing while the cloud cover, and presumed favorable breeze, lasted. In the minutes left it, the cloud would be continued in the same density.

Resisters would anticipate the "Fix bayonets" order, knowing that in making clubbing less effective by shielding with arms they would invite stronger measures. Monitors knew, as did the generals, that such shielding was useless against sharp blades. But resisters would continue to cry out when hurt, letting bayonet wielders know the pain they were inflicting. ANAVET defenders might try to be brave about getting injured, but not try to be stoics. Some might even have learned enough Axis X language to tell a soldier, "You are hurting me." Although ideally, "negating all violence" would mean standing firm no matter how much pain was inflicted, resisters would back up when wounded, but most would not retreat from gestures. If a soldier feigned jabs at a resister backing up too slowly or not at all, the latter would try to look the threatener in the eye but make no changes in bodily movement.

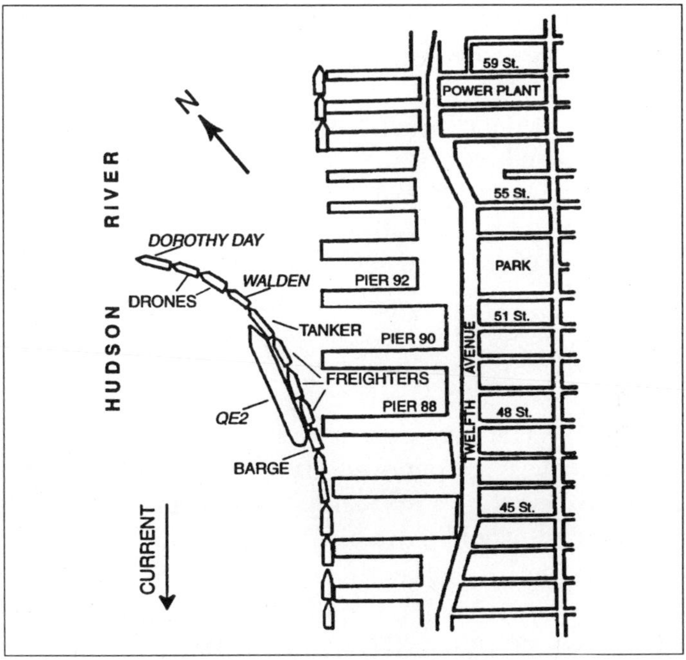

Figure C. The invader's troopship *Queen Elizabeth 2* is pulled away from docking piers while immersed in its smoke screen intended to hide civilian brutalities from photographers.

In the fast-moving, crowded action, monitors would have difficulty assisting the wounded to safety. In some cases victims might have to lie on deck until later, in peril of being trampled. Medical help for those extricated would be minimal, the city having no ambulance service during its continuing evacuation. Doctors would have been in place on piers and streets away from the smoke, possibly using tent hospitals. If world TV watchers could no longer see the action, they could see its bleeding results.

Soldiers reaching doors to the cabins, bridge, and below on each ship would search for crews to capture, but would find none. Like the power plant operators, crews were not resisters and would have left after tying their blockade vessel in place. But let us suppose some crews on blockade boats well upstream from the *QE2* were willing to help from a distance. Seeing the dense smoke they might improvise a stunt not in the script. At their signal resisters on piers would untie all blockading vessels alongside the *QE2* and four more upstream in the linkage.

Monitors would direct resisters to blockade only the ends of the four ships and barge and give full access for the surprised soldiers to the pier hawsers!

At that moment the lead ship would untie itself from the blockade vessel ahead of it and begin to pull the blockade string out into the Hudson River, the *QE2* with it. Were the smoke and other screens heavy enough, possibly only a *QE2* officer noticing its compass would be the first one aware of the innovative defense tactic. Troopship helicopters, which probably would have seen it first, soon would get orders to capture the towing boats by landing takeover crews on them. In the sketch (see Figure C), we assume two of these are operating with their regular civilian crews — the *Dorothy Day* and the *Walden* — while others in the towed linkage are drones, with vital operating parts such as diesel injection nozzles removed. The two crews would similarly remove such parts before surrendering to helicopter boarding parties. Not resisters, they would be treated as captured civilians under the Geneva Convention.

Until seized they and the downstream current could pull the *QE2* well away from its docking position. We may postulate that in the original planning of the blockade boats would have been linked with steel cable, so that even if troops were able to cut or untie the usual nylon hawsers to piers, they could do little about the linkage itself. Under tension from towing ships, such cables would be difficult to untie. In fact, even while still tied to piers such tension could have been provided by both *Dorothy Day* and *Walden*. Helicopters, then or now, would be wary of bombing such cable linkage lest a vessel sink and, as previously noted, become a blockade resting on the bottom of the Hudson. We can imagine acetylene equipment being lowered from the *QE2* to cut cabling, perhaps even before towing crews were captured. We can also imagine some freed freighters with both troops and resisters aboard carelessly drifting down the river. Such troops, mission accomplished to free freighters and no longer needing clubs and bayonets, would be awaiting further orders. Wounded resisters would be resting while others administered first aid. But the rest would be making good use of leaflets and PA horns with the captive audience. Some might even try to converse with the rather sheepish opposition.

5
Scenario: Resisters Block Streets and Hold Ground

At this point some reader might ask: Had the army somehow been able to machine gun all deck and pier resisters and dump their thousands of weighted corpses into the Hudson with no detection of any kind, would it not have done so? One reason against this would be that, as with the power plants, the army would need trained and experienced workers to run the city. Some of the energetic dock resisters could be the very employees wanted. We are not supposing the invaders are from some science fiction spaceship with their own mysterious supply of food, drinking water, heat, illumination, and other necessities. More than this, Axis X occupation troops would want convenient hotels, meals, street transportation, recreation, etc. The generals might be willing to be delayed many hours in docking — perhaps half a day — to gain some measure of cooperation from a subjugated population. Conquerors want workers, not corpses.

Many of history's mass slaughters of civilians have occurred in wartime when the victims were suspected of aiding the enemy or secretly using weapons themselves, or often they are killed in exaggerated retribution for the murder of an officer, etc. The previously-mentioned Amritsar massacre which convinced Gandhi to oppose Britain rather than cooperate was of this last type. Three Englishmen had been murdered and General Dyer was determined to teach the Indians a lesson.

His riflemen continued firing into the unarmed assembly until 379 were dead. Although there was no war in India itself, Britain was involved in World War I.

Most, perhaps all, of the gassings in Nazi death camps came after the start of World War II, and because of wartime secrecy, even many Germans living nearby did not realize what was happening. When shown a camp afterwards, one local Mayor committed suicide. Atrocities not secret may be minimized. When President Truman announced the atomic bombing of Hiroshima he termed that city a "military target." But with only a few soldiers and a military academy, Hiroshima had no military importance. Up until the 40th anniversary of the obliteration, domestic news media still referred to the fictional "military target." One might assume that today's neo-Nazis would capitalize on the Nazi gassings, saying in effect, "Beware, Jews, sex perverts, communists, and labor leaders! See what may happen to you!" But no. Instead right-wing hate groups attempt to prove the death camps never existed!

In more modern times a rather extraordinary example of trying to hide facts was the June 1989 massacre in Tiananmen Square, Beijing. Because the victimized students had been unable to keep the enormous support crowd nonviolent, the army retaliated by wiping out the demonstration. Although an army was the victimizer, the "Democratic Uprising" was aimed at the demonstrators' own government, not a foreign oppressor. At first the government denied the atrocity ever happened.

Axis X would hope, as had China, that there would be little or no boycott of itself by an enraged world. Even more than cooperation by New Yorkers, it would need the cooperation of other countries in continuing to supply vital imports and in buying Axis X exports. Remembering the UN-sponsored trade sanctions against Iraq in 1990, Axis X would be wary of any massacre it could not keep hidden. Already, the army's machine-gunning on the Verrazano Bridge had elicited more angry reaction than the home government wanted.

A more important reason for not carrying out a massacre would be the ANAVET stance of these Manhattan civilians. Gandhi, answering the objection "Hitler knows no pity. Your spiritual effort will avail nothing before him," replied, in part, in his newspaper: "Hitherto he and his likes have built upon their invariable experience that [people] yield to force. Unarmed men, women, and children offering nonviolent resistance without any bitterness will be a novel experience for them. Who can say it is not in their nature to respond to the higher and finer forces? They have the same soul that I have."[1]

Gandhi's comment on "their nature" applies even more to the multitude of subordinates in the field carrying out the orders of an occasional psychopathic dictator at the top.

A severe test for New York's resisters could occur if they were deliberately fired upon at close range. Would they still "negate all violence" by refusing to hate, spit, shout curses, make obscene gestures — while still refusing soldiers' orders? And, perhaps very angrily, still reprimanding their attackers? The faith of the ANAVET volunteer would be that first some soldiers, then more, might fire down at feet, or return to where they began — firing warning shots into the air. Some might become brave enough, or nauseated enough, not to fire at all.

Even in battle the percentage of combat troops who are unable to kill is surprisingly high. Studies after World War II revealed that only twelve to twenty-five percent of U.S. infantrymen who were in a position to fire at the enemy were able to pull the trigger. Training to remove the inhibition raised the percentage in the Korean War to only fifty percent. Let us now assume that the *QE2*, after the long-delaying tactics of resisters, would eventually dock alongside Pier 90 of the Passenger Ship Terminal, the three other troopships waiting at anchor downstream. The towed blockade linkage may have caught on the liner's bow before being severed, and during the delay the favorable downstream tide selected by the captain may have changed. The unwieldy ship, with no tug assistance, might suffer some collision damage.

The deck of the pier at this time might be some seven feet above water. Set back from its narrow walkway would be the corrugated steel doors of a two-story superstructure which open for freight. On the floor above are glass doors for passengers. The roof, edged by a low wall and with ramps to street, provides vehicle parking. Most troops would debark from their thirteen-story *QE2* on this roof. Resisters with their PA horns and posters — updated to announce the number of countries joining the trade boycott — would be in place on all three levels.

As the troopship drew alongside the pier it would probably fire light shells to blast open the steel doors to unload heavy equipment such as jeeps, crates, etc. Were there no warning, nearby resisters could be killed. Axis X might admit some "collateral damage." Gangways would then be extended to the pier's low deck, near hawser cleats, but instead of a smoke screen as at the aborted blockade landing attempt, there would be tear gas. Whereas it had to be avoided on blockade ships as a hazard to soldiers searching below decks, here on the relatively open pier the lethal dangers would be less.

The gas would drive away resisters blocking cleats, where masked sailors would tie up the *QE2*. Lines of masked soldiers would file down the gangways carrying long hoses whose nozzles would soon spew out noxious fumes. Were the gas diphenylamine, monitors would announce the gas was "DM," which causes no permanent injuries — only choking and eye burning, sneezing, and some vomiting.

Monitors would continue with reminder instructions for an orderly retreat: "Try to remain in your affinity group. Close eyes. Handkerchief over nose with left hand, right arm over neighbor's shoulder, walk backwards. Rows farthest from gas leave room for retreat for rows closer to it." The big open parking area with few obstructions would be ideal for a retreat which hopefully would be orderly as in practice sessions. On the bottom pier level, the deck where gas had already been used and steel doors blasted open, resisters would open the big doors on the opposite side. Were gas used on the pier's middle level, resisters would similarly ventilate by opening all glass doors.

What happens on these two enclosed levels would depend on the wind. Were it strong and blowing the gas back towards the troops, resisters might remain with their signs and horns for a long time. But in heavy gas there would be no row-by-row orderly retreat. Instead, affinity groups inside the structure would probably temporarily break up, paired individuals escaping as best they could. Were the wind unfavorable, this might happen at the first sign of gas. Monitors would be responsible in the regrouping to account for all members. Some rescue boats would be near the opposite side of the pier from the *QE2* to rescue resisters trapped by gas on the narrow deck walkway.

Using handkerchiefs might be considered a small breach of an ideal of complete vulnerability. In ANAVET the struggle is not weapon vs. weapon, as in warfare, but person vs. person or, more specifically, will vs. will. Compared to a gas mask, the common handkerchief or scarf is far from a piece of defense equipment. We need only observe a crowd encountering a bad odor to see that cloths held to noses is a normal reaction. Dry cloth itself filters little, and wet cloth only slightly more if some gas ingredients are water soluble, as ammonia; or reactive, as sulfur dioxide. Probably the chief function of a cloth is to keep out some bad air and keep in some exhaled for rebreathing. Palestinian civilians learned to breathe an onion's odor when gassed, presumably to increase protective tear flow. But as onions are not ordinarily carried as one's personal paraphernalia, ANAVET resisters would probably have decided not to use them.

The generals observing the stubborn rows of coughing, sneezing men and women might feel more exasperation than admiration for enemy tenacity. The slow takeover of three levels of the over 300 yards-long pier would be consuming enormous quantities of gas mostly intended for later use on city streets. After hoses from the ship were unreeled to full length the soldiers would have to use canisters. Replacements, until jeeps were unloaded, would need to be passed along by hand.

In war college the generals might have read of the amazing tenacity in World War II of Japanese soldiers trapped in hot jungles who chose to die painfully from flame throwers rather than surrender; of the tenacity of Soviet soldiers defending Nazi-besieged Leningrad. Did the generals remember that in the bitter cold of devastated Leningrad there were also tenacious and courageous civilians, that 900,000 starved and froze to death rather than see their city surrender? Did the generals remember the comparatively milder sacrifices of London's population during weeks of continuous nights of the Nazi blitz? Perhaps they forgot how, contrary to German expectations, the British were willing to see London destroyed rather than surrender?

Well before the last resister would have backed off the pier, or been helped or carried off, the *QE2*'s helicopters would have relayed pictures back of the advance's next obstacle: blockaded streets. Operation Car Block would have been a timing problem for the resistance because all cars and streets were needed for the evacuation. When the *QE2* first neared the piers, the adjacent Twelfth Avenue would most likely still be carrying capacity evacuee traffic. Fortunately the resistance delaying tactics would have given time for traffic to be diverted to parallel Ninth Avenue and other avenues beyond. Blocking would begin at the bases of all three of the big piers, filling all contiguous waterfront space and extending on streets north, east, and south. Over half a mile of 11th and 12th Avenues, and 46th to 54th Streets would be solid with cars. A news helicopter might be broadcasting from a safe distance:

> We see a jagged, herringbone pattern with two opposite rows of diagonally parked cars meeting in the center of each street. They are not bumper-to-bumper but offset sideways and overlapping to eliminate low, over-the-bumper jumping by soldiers. So they have

to climb over instead of jumping across roofs, the rows have a space between them. And the hoods are all raised.

In setting up the blockade drivers would park, set hand brakes, and remove distributor caps and wires. In the nighttime rush there would be many fender benders, but drivers could afford to be fast instead of careful because the Department of ANAVET National Defense would reimburse them for damages. Many cars which the invaders would blast out of the jam, or roll away to dump into the Hudson because other space was lacking for so many, would be worthless. Gas tanks, left draining, would be a hazard.

Included inside the blockaded streets would be DeWitt Clinton Park, two blocks up from Pier 90 on the other side of Twelfth Avenue. The next objective after the pier, the park would serve as a campground for landed troops. Comprising two city blocks, its grounds would be only partially blockaded because of slopes, playground and picnicking equipment, iron bar fences, restrooms, and granite outcroppings. Other troops would camp on the pier's roof, or inside as space permitted. At both sites all electricity and gas would be turned off, as would water except for the equivalent flow of one drinking fountain in the park.

Because most water and all food and camp items would have to be transported from ship to park, Twelfth Avenue to the waterfront would need clearing for both vehicles and foot soldiers. With the latter working in masks, stopping during occasional dynamitings, car removal would go slowly. As clearing progressed, rolls of razor wire, with guards stationed on the troops' side, would replace gas to keep resisters away. If we assume darkness has fallen, floodlights from portable generators and helicopters would illuminate the resisters' side, including nearby low buildings, as a precaution against ambushes and snipers. Resisters would welcome the floodlighting of their signs. Those near interpreters might venture close to the rolls, holding out empty hands and asking a guard on the other side, "May we talk with you?" This might happen especially in quiet spots where big PA horns had just been shot out.

The guards, ordered not to converse — not even to say "No" to such a question — would be embarrassingly vulnerable. Ordered to stand facing the enemy, to keep eyes and ears open, they could read signs and hear. With many horns blaring around the park and pier all night long, the resistance too, might feel it had a problem. Sleep, like food and water, is a human necessity. Some might ask, "Is preventing your adversary from sleeping a violation of ANAVET?" Others might reply, "Their guns make more noise than our horns they're knocking out." Probably the consensus would be that soldiers could always return to the ship.

This, in fact, would happen. Medics who ran out of sleeping pills could order men back to the *QE2*. Many soldiers, who for days had endured the jammed troopship and had hoped for land, might now be glad to return from the turmoil ashore. Luckiest would be those sent below deck where officers had cabins. Even there, with portholes and windows still closed tight against earlier gas, all might hear the horns even if not able to make out the words so clearly heard by soldiers on deck, on the pier, and in the park: "Iraq says gold, not peace, reason for invasion" or "South Africa joins boycott against Axis X."

But the sleep of many would be disturbed not by noise but by unwanted recollections of the day's grotesquely one-sided brutalities — clubbings, bayoneting, and gassings — inflicted on civilians who bore neither weapons nor hate.

Meanwhile the invasion's brass, the generals and admirals aboard the three other troopships waiting at anchor off Manhattan's lower tip, would study alternative landing sites. At first impatient over the long delaying of the *QE2* by the ship blockade and its cutting loose, they would now see that there would always be more delays at the big Terminal even with the blockade gone. On every pier there would be continued gassing of an enemy who refused to scatter, and all surrounding streets were fast being blocked as the need for evacuation routes lessened and as more cars became available. Obviously the plan to cut Manhattan in two from a single landing was impractical. Even the chutists at the seized power plant on the waterfront four blocks up from Clinton Park were still unrelieved; still dependent on helicopters for food and drink, for themselves and any dummy staff still held captive.

The brass would also be thinking of morale aboard the waiting ships. Soldiers were no longer confined below deck; the brass had decided that even though some leaflets would land on decks no matter how many drone planes were shot down, and were read, they could be refuted. This would have to be done anyway after the troops debarked — as would soon be happening at Pier 90 and Clinton Park. One leaflet showered on those sites and on all four troopships showed pictures of a woman pulled down to the pavement by her hair, and a man wincing from a bayonet wound. Briefing officers would explain the victims were suspected of carrying grenades.

Examining maps and weighing alternatives, the brass would decide to make a second landing in Battery Park, near the anchored ships and conveniently near two government vaults where tritium might be stored. The Treasury's Assay Office and the New York Federal Reserve Bank were only blocks away. Their opening could be started immediately, the thousands of tanks of acetylene and oxygen having to be hauled only short distances once ashore. (Original plans had been for conveyor unloading at piers if necessary, using ships' electricity.) The long waterfront, too shallow for liners and hence unblockaded, also has no structures to hamper debarking as with the *QE2*. Troops could be shuttled to the low bulkhead in lifeboats, and tanks of cutting gas and other heavy equipment landed in the flat park by helicopter.

With Battery Park, ten times larger than Clinton, as the main encampment, troops could then march up Broadway less than a mile to City Hall and declare Manhattan to be occupied. Troops from a new encampment in City Hall Park would join those from Battery and Clinton Parks, and from Pier 90 and the *QE2*, to control the area up to 79th Street. Hopefully, surrender terms would be signed, stopping all street blocking, and allowing as many banks as desired to be "inspected."

To allow the enemy as little advance warning as possible the landing operation would start at 3 A.M., twenty minutes after a diversionary assembly at Clinton. But the satellites of UN observers and the U.S. Department of ANAVET Defense take no rest, and would have no trouble seeing the lowering of gangways and lifeboats on the hindsides of the three anchored ships. Flotilla blockade boats might be the last to notice the activity because of glare on the water from their now illuminated signs. Also, Axis ships might have a nighttime policy of machine gunning, instead of upsetting by helicopter wash, any which came too close, claiming they posed possible underwater bomb threats.

Keeping at a distance because of gunning would obviously be compromising "negating all violence" — resisters not altering behavior because of violence or of its threat. But ANAVET organizers could point out that soon there would be no reduction of posters and amplifiers, which were now being transferred to expendable rafts. These would drift with the current, close to the ships, and those surviving gunfire would be rounded up beyond the forbidden area. When the tide shifted they would drift by again. In time all rafts would be of heavy wood to better survive machine gunning, so that banners and PA equipment would be the main items replaced. This raft parade, changing directions twice daily, would continue as long as the ships were there.

But when the lifeboats began leaving, filled with troops bound for Battery Park, all firing in their direction would end. Flotilla boats could then race into the forbidden area to greet oncoming troops. The army would respond by again upsetting the resisters with helicopters. But because the many flotilla boats would outnumber the helicopters, many resisters would get through to face-to-face contacts with soldiers. Some resister crews would discover that lifeboat waves smoothed out waves made by helicopters, and that when a small craft could get close to a bigger lifeboat it was not easily upset. We can imagine an outboard inflatable almost touching the high gunwale of a lifeboat and a resister reaching up to hand leaflets to nearby soldiers. We can imagine their motor shot dead before any hesitant soldiers accepted one, but that some leaflets fall near soldiers and get read.

If there were an interpreter aboard such a close resister boat he/she might stand and give an unamplified message face-to-face. If the small boat were riddled by bullets, jettisoning its outboard motor would give the resisters a still-floating hull for support. Perhaps some soldiers might glance back at the survivors bobbing in the wake. Yet if a lieutenant ordered "Eyes front," there would be big banners to read on the curved shoreline ahead. Beyond the floodlit, hand-held banners would be hoards of resisters crowding in front of cars being parked to blockade all of Battery Park.

When the lead lifeboats would be some two hundred yards offshore the helicopters overtaking them would blare the warning that drums of tear gas would be dropped along the waterfront, with the usual "no one moving out of the way will in any way be injured." Aware that overhead observers could see objects falling on the park itself, well lit by headlights of both parked and arriving cars, the army would try to drop the drums only on the water. Any resisters' boats would scurry away from the one-third-mile park waterfront.

Impact would release greater quantities than previously used for crowd control but the resisters' ex-army advisors might already have advised that Battery Park's open terrain, unlike the piers, would make aerial gas bombing more feasible, and that landings from boats would make it desirable. Monitors would have arranged for possible fast evacuation instead of previous slow retreating. Advisors might also have pointed out that the big grass-and-tree park would be first another campsite rather than thoroughfare. Thus carblocking would not be the sophisticated herringbone pattern blocking troop movement. Rather, aisles would be left from the fifty-five-foot-wide waterfront promenade all the way to surrounding streets. Troops would still have to remove cars to make camp.

We may assume that after the monitors call for rapid evacuation there may be minor injuries. Headlights would help the exiting, but because the cars parked as they arrived, the glare would be against outgoing resisters. Were there more casualties than resisters could carry to safety, volunteer medics *in masks* could be asked to help. We should assume city evacuation may still have precedence over normal traffic and there is not yet any regular ambulance service. But as noted about that evacuation, others besides trained resisters chose to stay. Some of these braver residents might have volunteered as medical helpers.

A smoke bombing would follow the gas bombing to prevent all but the most sophisticated picture taking. Troops arriving in their lifeboats would machine gun whatever empty boats might be blockading the twenty-foot depth at the waterfront. The sunken debris would slow but not prevent soldiers from reaching and climbing the seven-foot bulkhead to the top of the low wall edging the park's paved promenade.

The landing troops would start rolling cars into the water and smashing iron fences and railings that were in the way. Soldiers would be in masks which, along with the park's many trees, would add to the exhausting work of clearing the area for privies, field kitchens, portable generators, tents and sleeping bags.

Eventually the Battery Park area would resemble that of DeWitt Clinton: five-foot rolls of razor wire around the perimeter, guards inside, resisters outside trying to converse, blaring horns and big signs on buildings bordering the park, the lingering odor of tear gas, and a trickle of running water for some twenty thousand soldiers.

Because the invader would by now have been successful in using tear gas to establish two bases in Manhattan, we can assume resisters might reconsider ANAVET policy of not using masks. Let us assume an emergency session with the Secretary of ANAVET defense and hundreds of resisters. After much discussion the no-mask policy would continue for the usual reasons. First, the invader would otherwise escalate to more injurious weapons like cattle prods, rubber or real bullets or, as on the blockade boats where gas could not be used, bayonets. Second, ANAVET resisters should remain vulnerable, appealing to an opponent's unwillingness to hurt helpless human beings, appealing to the best in an adversary. Masks change vulnerable humans into objects more suitable for attacking. Finally, only in military thinking does losing ground mean losing the battle. In nonviolent resistance yards lost on the ground are less important than millimeters advanced into the aggressor's mind.

After this reaffirmation of policy there would be less feeling of frustration because of the opportunity to reach soldiers' minds when they "marched" up Broadway to City Hall under a shower of leaflets that would rival any ticker tape parade of past decades.

The brass, still comfortably aboard an anchored troopship, would decide that aerial bombing of the car blockade up any street from Battery Park would be unmanageable, leaving too many craters, and loose glass overhead. Thus a masked Army Engineer Corps would start with small demolition charges, while the Infantry followed, piling the debris at curbs and posting guards in the cleared path. Progress at about one hundred yards per hour would be slow. As resisters foresaw, Broadway was selected as the most direct route with its least number of cars to remove.

No military strategists would have been more delighted to see an enemy walk into their trap than high up in Broadway buildings, showering leaflets on the workers below. Printing was in large type, so that those which stuck to uniforms and knapsacks could be read through masks. Elevators in buildings would have been disconnected after resisters reached the highest floors and non-resisters had left, operable only when resisters signaled building engineers. Soon the PA horns of army patrol helicopters would be echoing between the skyscrapers: "No one may appear at a window or on a roof. All windows must be tightly closed."

Refusing such orders, resisters would duck when helicopters sprayed bullets. The army would also have warned civilian aircraft not to fly within firing range of its airspace over Broadway. Photographs and videos could thus be taken only by satellites and by adventurous photographers defying orders to stay off roofs and away from windows. Picture taking would otherwise be advantageous because for security the army would have no smoke screen. Its guards and helicopters would be scrutinizing the scene for snipers and terrorists.

The possible presence of such would be a greater overall danger for ANAVET defense than for the army. Inside buildings the security against violent and zealous non-resisters would be a major concern. Any such attack on troops below would immediately be seized upon by Axis X to bolster its claim that the U.S. was armed and only waiting for the best moment to use its secret weapon. The army would also like an excuse to fire back with the overwhelming violence it was prepared to use. In fact, so valuable an advantage would be gained that the army itself might try to plant snipers to fire on its own soldiers. Troops might even have been deliberately ordered not to wear helmets, so desperate would Axis X be for some casualties of its own in a losing campaign for favorable world opinion. Resisters would try to be inside all openable windows, not only to drop leaflets (avoiding any bundles looking like bombs) but also to guard against anyone armed or trying to throw out chairs, books or other items.

Large-type leaflets, like others periodically floating down on the four ships, two parks, the pier, Twelfth Avenue and the waterfront, would have new content. One might be an update of a leaflet series featuring a number, such as: "Uzbekistan has become the seventy-eighth nation to join the total boycott of Axis X."

There would be excerpts from Uzbekistan's condemnation of the aggression as "brutal and based on obvious lies," etc. This might be followed by a list of the seventy-seven nations who had previously joined the boycott. Another leaflet might be a translation of ANAVET policy as stated in its succinct "4-H" form: "We will not Hurt you, Hate you, Help you, Heed you."

The clearing of the sixth-tenths mile of Broadway would strain the invader's stocks of demolition explosives, tear gas, and razor wire. Fresh supplies would have to be flown in from home bases. Planes, with no place to land, would need to parachute special floatable freight containers near the anchored ships, carrying only so much as would allow fuel for the flight home. There would be plenty of converted air liners for the shuttle, boycotting nations having banned all Axis X air commerce. Crews of the troopships would be busy retrieving the containers, hoisting them on deck for unpacking, then repacking for sending ashore via lifeboat and helicopter.

On Broadway, removal of car debris would continue to be slow. Where it is only four lanes wide, only two bulldozers could work behind the demolition team. Behind them, soldiers wearing masks and heavy gloves would pile the smoldering materials up against buildings along both sidewalks. This would block normal front door entrances, but resisters inside would be prepared to stay for long periods. Army horns would tell all occupants to wait until the gas ended, after which they would be told when to descend fire escapes to be escorted to safety. There would not be enough flashlights or time for soldiers to search buildings. Some who would be posted as guards along the "cleared" street might have private plans to get through the piled wreckage and broken front windows of cafes when gas permitted.

Because resisters would be waiting amongst the blockading cars on side streets to have close contacts after the gas dispersed, the army would resort to rolls of razor wire as at the parks, placed here on one side or the other of the rows of debris. Subway entrances on sidewalks could pose a problem: Should stairs be blocked to keep out resisters, or left open for army access to potential bomb shelters? Because the army would still believe the secret weapon allegation, tangles of razor wire would be pushed into stairways, retrievable to sidewalks but not easily removed by resisters below.

After some eleven hours, Broadway itself would be cleared enough for twenty thousand troops to march to City Hall Park. But these grounds too would need clearing for the massive assembly. About twice the area of DeWitt Clinton, but without the nearby water into which cars could be rolled, City Hall Park would have its car debris piled on the tops of cars blockading adjacent streets. An exception would be at the northeast corner of the triangular park, where a cleared passage would allow army access to the thirty-eight story Municipal Building across the street, the working center of city government.

Amidst lingering whiffs of gas, showers of self-adhesive leaflets, and the noise of guns aimed at open windows, troops would march up Broadway to City Hall Park. To impress on Manhattan's politicos that Axis X was an occupying power, as many as possible would fill the grounds, leaving space only for field kitchens and about fifty latrines just landed by helicopter. There would also be a permanent landing area for helicopters, where the generals from their ship quarters would now arrive, as announced, to sign an occupation contract with the City of New York.

There might be no more attempted resistance on the grounds or inside City Hall itself. Let us suppose that although most employees would have left, the Mayor and City Council Members have assembled to meet and denounce the interlopers. The latter might find no resistance to their entry. Instead, the usual inspector inside the front door might routinely ask the astonished generals for their briefcases for metal and drug detection. The lobby's two circular stairways might be crowded with reporters. At the information desk the generals' interpreter would be told the Mayor and Council Members were waiting upstairs.

There, in the big public room, the Mayor, President of the City Council, and its three dozen members might quietly and respectfully rise when the guests entered and invite them to be seated. We can imagine the general in command and his interpreters reading a business-as-usual surrender contract to be signed by city officials:

> Streets shall be cleared of all obstructions, and normal traffic resumed. Police, fire, and sanitation and other public employees, and all others working or otherwise functioning in the Occupied Zone, as defined below, shall continue as normally, observing the same routines, time schedules, etc. as previous to the occupation. All services, public or private, such as transportation, education, communication, news gathering and dissemination, broadcasting, banking and general commerce shall continue normally, subject only to changes agreed upon by the Board of Review of the Western Atlantic Peace Army, whose members are herein named. . . .

Up to this point city officials would have been listening attentively. But before the terms went on to billeting the army in hotels, the Mayor would rise to interrupt. Her/His Honor would declare that the city would sign no surrender terms, that no orders of any unwelcome invaders would be accepted or carried out. All requests for provisions, housing, etc. would be ignored. Any areas into which the invaders might try to expand would have no electricity, water, gas, or other services such as transportation or those provided by hotels, cafes and other businesses. Only exceptions would be police and fire departments, the latter getting water only in emergencies.

(In occupied areas the police would probably handle only civilians and, according to custom, let military police deal with army personnel. We can picture the city force armed as usual for dealing with law-breakers; although we can assume civilian life will improve as a result of disarmament for the many reasons stated in Chapter 1, I am not postulating some ideal society free of all crime. But during the five years of disarming since 2005, city employees and all government workers in the nation would have received enough ANAVET instruction to know there should be no sniping, bombing, sabotage, etc. of an invader's troops. Police now feeling unable so to act, or unable to enforce such conduct by others, could, if residing in the zone, join the evacuation.)

As the Mayor finished speaking, all lights and ventilation would go off and water would slow to a trickle. Assuming he/she makes no attempt to escape and is incarcerated, the location of the incarceration would be a problem for the army. Should it be in comfortable quarters in a ship's cabin, or inconveniently in the Mayor's office, supplied with officers' food, bottled ship water for drinking, bucketed bay water for flushing toilets? (Most government officials if held captive might cooperate as prisoners, but some might go on hunger strikes, as would be true for other trained resisters.)

The generals, hardly surprised by now at this intransigence, would already have planned seizure of the real center of city operations, the Municipal Building across the street. Soldiers would again don masks and start clearing adjacent streets. Others would start converting the park to Camp Number 3, there being no hoped-for hotel accommodations.

In the Municipal Building employees who were not ANAVET resisters would already have left. As at City Hall and the power plants, all records would have been computerized on discs and relocated to outside the zone. Army engineers would find no maps of Manhattan's six thousand miles of water piping with its 175,000 valves, no maps of subways, steam tunnels, underground electrical conduits, no names and addresses of Public Works employees. Leafletters who had been on high floors would probably accept army PA instructions to evacuate before tear gas is released, walking down as many as thirty floors on the building's steel, square spiral stairways, and then resisting outside. There, in the camera's eyes, they would refuse further orders, resisting clubs, bayonets, gas, as previously described.

Perhaps about this time, with soldiers strung out along long "frontiers" and only guards and razor wire between them and deserting, the resistance would start scattering a leaflet on bright orange paper printed on both sides. The message would be different from all previous ones:

> SAFE CONDUCT PASS FOR DEFECTORS
>
> Hold this card over your head in the sight of any civilian. Do not carry any weapons. You will be given transportation to a safe lodging and free food. You will be welcome to enjoy living in the United States for as long as you choose to remain.

The other side might read:

> Do not be deceived by your leaders. All vaults they plan to open here, and at Fort Knox, will be opened by the UN to prove there are no secret weapons, upon your withdrawal. The only weapons at Knox are guns for its guards. Brave soldiers willing to defend their country should not be degraded by orders to injure unarmed civilians. You can refuse to hurt us as we refuse to hurt you. You can choose to defect. We offer you sanctuary.

Assuming the army wanted subways for bomb shelters, securing them would begin immediately from station entrances at captured City Hall and Battery Parks. Because the system might still be evacuating residents, cutting off electricity by the defense would have to be highly selective. An army task force from City Hall Park walking the rails south (downtown) a quarter mile might find lighted platforms for both directions at Fulton Street Station, and patrons waiting to board. The lieutenant in command would announce that all service was ending and that people would have to use buses on the streets. Most patrons, rather frightened by the sight of troops, might have begun leaving even before the order. ANAVET resisters would remain, and others on the street learning of the troops' presence would descend stairways to the station. There on opposite platforms, facing two rows of soldiers between them but probably not yet having bullhorns or posters, resisters could call out phrases memorized in Axis X language: Troops are unwelcome invaders, should go home, refuse orders, etc.

The soldiers on the track level, having only rifles because gas would be too hazardous in subways, would be back-to-back facing resisters. The lieutenant in charge, alert for snipers and entrapment, might be tense. His English-speaking public relations officer might smile courteously as he recited his no-one-doing-as-directed-will-be-injured instructions. But none would leave, and more would be coming down from the street with posters and leaflets. One might arrive who knew the troops' language. She/he might come to the front of a platform and explain that they were not waiting for a train but were unarmed volunteers defending the station from capture. "*You* should leave because *you* don't belong here. This is *our* country. *We* belong here, not you."

The lieutenant might give them thirty seconds to leave, and order rifles raised. The resister spokesperson might urge the soldiers to refuse orders to fire on unarmed civilians, and/or urge their lieutenant to refuse orders to shoot uncooperative persons.

Exactly what happens then might depend on the presence of cameras. The lieutenant may have had permission to use real bullets "as necessary" because of the absence in the subway of media, UN, and other professional photographers. Any visible cameras might be the first targets but a resister with one, wanting soldiers to know they and their raised rifles were being photographed, might come to the front and openly take flash photos. Were any guns fired, the picture might show the smoke, even the flame. If the first shot was, as is common in such confrontations, a warning, it might be directed below the resisters at the vertical, four-foot face of the concrete platform, the raised height of resisters above soldiers.

Whether the shots splattered the concrete below or the station's tiles above, resisters would know the bullets were steel. If the photographer continued to take pictures, he/she might be shot. If the firing was caught on film, the fate of the camera would be important: The first photo of a soldier shooting an unarmed resister might be seen by nearly a billion people worldwide. The camera would be passed quickly, or in the well-lit station, thrown overhead to the rear and up to some street reporter. If the reporter had the right equipment, the picture on a light-proof computer disc could be transmitted immediately to the world by satellite.

We have assumed only one photographer on the ten-cars-long passenger platform, but even before any professionals arrived there would likely be home videos and other amateur equipment. Those distant from the action might be safer but find flash bulbs give inadequate lighting.

The photographer(s), and anyone else injured by the same bullet(s), would be helped to the street to receive medical attention, be interviewed, and photographed. Access to street level would involve long walks because both nearby Broadway exits would be blocked by razor wire, as previously mentioned; resisters would use passenger walkways to neighboring Nassau Street. When possible, monitors would try to get rescue volunteers down to subway level.

If there were injuries, resisters would move forward to fill spaces. An unsure lieutenant probably would order the strained soldiers to rest from their firing positions, and perhaps confer with his public relations officer about the next move. In the confrontation it would be crucial for resisters to screen their own group, monitors keeping out possible zealous patriots, non-ANAVET resisters who might be tempted to throw a bottle over those ahead. Training for resisters would have included the lesson of Sharpeville, South Africa, where some seven thousand Africans massed at a gate in a nonviolent demonstration in 1960. Police tried to disperse them with gas, but they fell back only thirty paces. Armored cars and planes then unsuccessfully tried to intimidate the orderly and disciplined crowd. The impasse lasted several hours. Then a few demonstrators threw rocks at the police. Without warning the police opened fire, killing sixty-seven men, women, and children, and wounding many more. This led to work stoppages, which led to arrests and the government's reign of terror.

Resisters would know that rocks can rightly be considered lethal weapons. Israel declared them so and authorized its troops to shoot Palestinian stone-throwers. But in any impasse with an adversary, resisters themselves would have no time to be impatient for "action." All would be too busy trying to communicate with, and otherwise educate, the opposition. In the subway there would also be the orange-colored offers of help to troubled soldiers wanting a way out of their degrading situation.

If some irresponsible bottle-throwing by uninvited persons in the rear did occur, and exasperated soldiers began a massacre, what number of casualties would monitors decide was an unacceptable figure, to use a military term, before deciding to retreat? Ten dead and dying? Sixty-seven as at Sharpeville? Three hundred seventy-nine as at Amritsar? Such figures would have been too minuscule to notice in anti-nuke discussions of past decades. As far as anyone could tell, the U.S. was prepared to "accept" tens of millions of its own dead in any nuclear exchange with the then USSR, and hundreds of millions worldwide.

Let us assume there is no breakdown of ANAVET policy, either by impatient patriots — or by provocateurs, as happened in Vietnam war protests. Army tensions would still be building as resisters came onto the station's other platform and soldiers had to face two ways from tracks in the middle. The lieutenant might well decide to call for reinforcements, more troops and/or supplies of rubber bullets and stun guns, knowing that at the City Hall Park entry, troops might take half an hour to assemble and then walk the quarter mile of tracks in the dark. While waiting the lieutenant might order occasional warning shots, but more likely he would have his soldiers retire into the dark tunnel, away from the "enemy propaganda."

His request might be treated several ways at his City Hall base:

1. Four hundred armed infantry would be sent.
2. Same, but without stun guns (as batteries were needed for flashlights).
3. Same as 2, but without rubber bullets (now needed on streets during gas shortages).
4. No soldiers or weapons could be spared (because needed elsewhere).

This last seems the most probable. A higher priority would be the scouring of the Municipal Building for information needed to operate the city (although it would turn out to be a futile task). Also, fears of secret weapons attacks would be lessening with the lapse of time. With so many Manhattanites continuing to remain in the city, many soldiers and officers would increasingly come to believe what resisters were saying. The lieutenant might well be ordered to withdraw and to cut the third rail with thermite bombs to prevent resumption of train service. Resisters on the platforms would applaud, their interpreters explaining to the soldiers that the cheering was for the decision to leave, lest it seem the resisters were celebrating a victory.

But even were there no such retreat, if reinforcements had come and resisters were driven out, Axis X and its army would have learned again that the *threat* of violence has no power, that it has to be *used.* Soldiers ordered to use that violence against brave and harmless civilians would eventually realize, according to ANAVET psychology, that they have been debased into being cowardly bullies. It would be as if a matador, conditioned to risking his life in the bull ring and still in his prime, discovered he had been assigned to a slaughterhouse. How long would it take him to say about his job, "This is not for me"?

6
Scenario: Pressure Placed on Invading Army

At the end of several days the invaders may have occupied, as mentioned: four isolated power plants; one passenger ship terminal pier on the Hudson, adjacent DeWitt Clinton Park; and a connecting street passage in Battery Park and two lanes up Broadway six-tenths of a mile, to City Hall and the surrounding park; and the adjacent Municipal Building. One troopship would be at the pier, with three others anchored downstream.

Troops not still aboard ships would be camping in the three parks and on the pier. Lower grade officers might be housed in unlit and unheated, two-story City Hall. Upper echelons would remain more comfortably aboard, commuting as necessary by helicopter to cramped landing spots in the camps. Food for those ashore would be prepared partly on ships and partly in field kitchens.

For most army personnel ashore the fragrance of coffee brewing and food cooking would be mixed with whiffs of burning fuel, lye from privies, occasional tear gas and, especially along Broadway, of urine. Sounds would include resisters' loudspeakers and occasional shots to knock them out, an army PA system with patriotic songs, the muffled roar of portable motor generators and, at Battery Park, the blasting of automobiles in the water to make room for lifeboats landing supplies. More food, fuel, blankets, tents, lye, camp stoves, flashlights, matches, soap, laundry tubs, tear gas, and razor wire would be brought by ships, supplementing airlift-parachuting. Tankers would be en route with replacement power plant fuel and with experienced operators, there being no jet runways for airlifting personnel. All supplies would have to come from Axis X itself, no stops en route being possible because of the boycott, which also would mean supplies at home would be low. Axis X might not be able to buy any more tear gas, or certain necessary ingredients, or canisters to hold it, etc.

Over time the resisters' PA horns would probably not be blaring as continuously as at first. Resisters would have continued discussing the line between "educating" and "harassing," tired themselves of the noise of horns and answering rifle fire. It was obvious that only a few sleepless camping soldiers could now be returned even temporarily to the relative quiet of a ship.

Let us assume the consensus of monitors and their affinity groups would be shown in a PA announcement each night: "It is now 10:30 P.M. For the remainder of your sleeping night we shall make no loud announcements which might disturb your rest. We do not want to intimidate you as individual persons, for as persons you are our friends.

"We also want you to have clear minds tomorrow to think about important questions, such as, Do I now believe my government's claim that there are secret weapons in the United States? Should I injure people who are willing to suffer, but not to injure me, in defending their country?"

The good night message would remind not only soldiers but resisters that while ANAVET policy was to make the invasion difficult, it was not to harm people. While the army would be forced to import its own food, no off-duty individual soldier asking resisters for food would be turned away hungry.

The last question of the sign-off announcement would draw attention to injuring. In King's civil rights campaigns those hurt did not stoically try to hide the fact but openly let aggressors know there was pain. As a Christian minister, King was fond of saying, "unearned suffering is redemptive" in explaining nonviolent action to reporters. Many Christians will see in this philosophy a relationship to the theology that Jesus' sacrifice on the cross was for the redemption of humankind. Gandhi ranked this transforming power of suffering above that of reason alone in converting an opponent. If correct, then the suffering of resisters would be more important than their signs, leaflets, and horns in lowering the fighting morale of the soldiers.

Outside the occupied areas all immediate streets would be car-blocked. Those farther away might still be evacuating residents, or returning earlier evacuees now wishing to check on homes and belongings. According to prepared plans, many of them might have left their living quarters and all food to specified resisters. Other evacuees, seeing no bombardment of Manhattan and hearing of no atrocities against non-resisters, might decide to come home and try staying awhile. Like their courageous neighbors, they too would take their chances on having to move out if their area became occupied and was without water, electricity, or gas. In the meantime, they, like their neighbors, would share food left behind. If some of their own was so used, they would know that the Department of ANAVET Defense would fully reimburse them. A nation no longer spending 300 billion dollars every year on violent defense but now enjoying the new prosperity resulting from a balanced budget, with no national debt or interest to pay, could easily afford the few billions that nonviolent defense would cost.

Life outside the perimeter of blocked streets could become fairly normal. Trucks would begin to supply Manhattan's many corner grocery stores and delicatessens. Two-way traffic on the Brooklyn Bridge would be restored, its ramps near City Hall Park would remain closed but those on the FDR Drive, running down the east side of Manhattan would be open. Much of the subway system outside the cut-rail section could be back to normal.

The entire razor-wire perimeters of occupied areas would be closely surrounded by resisters. We might assume a cross-section of such a boundary to be, from the inside out:

Camping soldiers

Sentries

Razor wire (five-foot diameter rolls)

Resisters (standing one- to three-hour shifts)

Bombed car wreckage

Buildings and blocked streets

Each affinity group and its monitor would make its own compromise with "negating all violence" in reacting to a sentry's "anyone touching the wire will be shot!" A group translator might ask, "If one of us touches, will you shoot to kill? Or only injure?" The purpose would not be to probe physical limitations so much as to probe the thinking of the sentry. Undoubtedly under orders not to engage in conversation, the guard might not reply, but this would not end the resister's attempts. Nearby soldiers would overhear, and possibly some prohibited dialogue might ensue. In this case hidden news cameras, catching every happening along the boundary, would be detrimental rather than helpful to the defense; soldiers willing, even eager, to talk with civilians could be intimidated by fear of being identified in news photos, and punished. Resisters would need to be aware of this and make allowances. They might suggest to such soldiers, where a guard would be sympathetic, that both resisters and soldiers could pretend they were not conversing. This would be a situation where establishing the soldiers' trust in the "enemy" might be aided by deceit!

Breaks in the morale of the invader would probably begin in the lowest ranks. After these few days in New York, some officers would see that the courteous but determined resisters were not going to be frightened, and were as brave and willing to be hurt as any soldier. Commanding officers would realize this war was one of wills: troops, with their overwhelming physical power, trying to break the will of the populace, and the latter, believing in the moral force of their righteous cause, trying to break the will of the troops.

What would be important for troop morale would be action, something new, something fresh. With all streets potentially car-blocked and no surrender agreement forthcoming, and with no foreseeable army means to continue doing so, let us suppose the brass would next try to expand its hold with a third waterfront landing and campsite at East River Park, downstream from the still-unrelieved 79th Street plant. We may assume the army would have reached the two gold vaults near Battery Park, and possibly other banks near Broadway, but still plans to include all others and power plants below a 79th Street boundary.

The three anchored ships with their remaining troops would move around the tip of Manhattan and up the East River as far as they could go to the Brooklyn Bridge. From there, troops would be shuttled to the waterfront of the long, narrow park. The landing would repeat Battery Park, but with two major differences: First, to prevent carblocking, helicopters in a surprise raid would shoot out tires of all cars on the F.D.R. Drive bordering the long, narrow park. The ground level freeway would be the only access for cars onto the grass and walks of the park. The second difference would be that because tear gas would probably be exhausted by now, and batteries for stun guns in short supply, the army would experiment with napalm — not yet used but still plentiful — for repelling resisters from the park.

The helicopter attack on the Drive's fast traffic would cause many injuries, even fatalities. Pilots might fire only at tires at close range — flying as low as possible above pedestrian overpasses. They might even give warnings to fire only at tires of moving vehicles, saying that no persons leaving parked vehicles would be hurt. The army would know this assurance was only for world opinion, that even if only tires were shot, traffic mishaps from sudden braking and careening could be serious. Assume the tactic served its intent, that traffic entering each end of the targeted section slowed to a congested stop and all vehicles were abandoned, that the Drive was carblocked against the resisters before they could carblock the park.

While many helicopters were still active up and down the Drive, others would make the opposite side of the park a flaming waterfront. Done in early morning hours when the fewest people were around, the row of napalm bombs along the promenade would be dropped carefully, so cameras would see that persons were not burned but only driven back by the heat. Because of the surprise there might not be any small blockading craft, but anyone aboard a nearby boat would be similarly driven back from the flaming waterfront. People in the park watching from a comfortable distance would soon be driven farther west by a second wall of napalm laid alongside the first. This would continue until the last strip filled the entire park, forcing its relatively few visitors to escape via the Drive's pedestrian overpasses.

Meanwhile troops in an armada of lifeboats, timed to arrive at the promenade when cool enough to occupy, would have left the anchored ships. They would climb the seven-foot bulkhead, and lifeboats would return for a second load, arriving back when the second strip of blackened grass and trees was cool enough to occupy. In this manner a new but very sooty campground might be occupied by say twenty-two thousand troops with no gassing, clubbing, or bayoneting of civilians, no blasting of blockading cars. In its campaign for world opinion, Axis X would try to make a virtue of its necessity to use napalm. But in the water we could assume a rougher treatment of resisters than in the shuttle to Battery Park. Because helicopters would be needed for shooting tires and dropping napalm, there could be fewer upsettings of resisters' boats and more gunning of those coming too close. In reporting to its own citizens, Axis X would term these deaths as "collateral damage."

In spite of losing another beachhead, and with little opportunity to resist, ANAVET defenders would seize the new opportunity to win the hearts and minds of soldiers. Unlike Battery and City Hall Parks and Broadway, bordered mostly with office buildings, the high structures across the FDR Drive from the new campground would be apartments. Many of the families who had not left in the original evacuation would now decide that the machine gunning and napalm had come too close and it was time to leave. But many might choose to stay longer, yet not want PA horns and banners to attract rifle fire. Resisters, rarely wanting brave residents to be idle, would work out a safe way for them to participate. On the ground both resisters and others could fly eight-foot kites which, when the wind was westerly, would go far out over the camp. Of nonflammable material, they would not be vulnerable to incendiary bullets. Some, hovering low, would have big letters. Others, higher, would carry leaflets and release mechanisms, and be pulled in after the load was dumped. Unlike parachuting bundles from high altitude drone planes, replacement costs would be minimal. When a kite was shot down, its cargo would often scatter where desired.

Educational leaflets would, from the beginning, be designed to be interesting reading as well as challenging. The newest figure of the number of countries boycotting Axis X could be placed alongside a terse quote from that newest nation condemning the invasion. One foreign office, for example, might ridicule the claim that the UN's Disarmament Verification Commission could not know if the United States had nuclear missiles on hidden mobile launchers — all supplied of course by tritium from New York and Knox. Because of soot, leaflets would not be sticky.

News of any desertions would also make good copy. Let us assume that by now one or more soldiers would have defected, perhaps taking advantage of the offers on the orange card by swimming from one of the waterfront camps or from a boat en route. On a leaflet an interview with a reporter would need no translation: "They say we'll all use bayonets because there's no more gas, and on civilians that seems stupid because there ought to be a better way to find out if there are secret weapons over here."

We are assuming Axis X has as good a wartime news control as any modern nation today, that all information via phone, computer, FAX, etc. is well censored. If we assume the technical ability to jam incoming radio and TV would be even better than at present, we can also assume that sending techniques will have improved, so that there would always be listeners in Axis regions able to hear some bands at some times for contraband news. College students could well be the first to demand more information about various rumors. If they risked hanging signs from dorm windows or otherwise displayed "enemy propaganda" posters in public, satellite news pictures of it would be passed along to occupation troops by Manhattan's resisters — as of course would any news of Axis arrests aimed at tightening its censorship.

Much more hidden in the Axis might be a some pervasive uneasiness about war dispatches. The "East River victory" could claim to establish control over Manhattan, now from the east, from the west (Hudson), from the south (Battery Park) and centrally (City Hall area). But available maps would show that the newly-won park extended no farther north than 14th Street, sixty-five blocks short of the previously captured but now unmentioned, power plant on 79th Street. Uneasiness would grow as more realized their wartime shortages were in part due to UN sanctions.

Although the UN on the riverfront between 42nd and 46th Streets was well north of the new encampment, many of its eleven thousand commuting employees would be inconvenienced by the carblocking on its East River Drive portion. The autonomous body, on its international site and not part of Manhattan's defense, would be working to make its boycott more effective. It might help nations dependent on the Axis for certain items to obtain them from other sources, while poorer, importing nations might be granted subsidies if this alternate source were more expensive.

Because of such efforts the squeeze could come quicker than it did in Iraq in 1990. There, four months after its aggression began, sanctions were ninety-five percent effective against exports and ninety percent against imports. Unfortunately, President George Bush decided that sanctions alone would not work and sent troops. But given time, sanctions can be effective; those of the United States alone cost the South African economy some $30–$40 billion during the 1980s.

Here it is important to note that an international boycott against an aggressor, while valuable, need not be a necessity. There were no such trade sanctions against Britain during India's satyagraha campaign to rid itself of a centuries-old occupation. Indian consumers boycotted British cloth enough to cripple Lancashire mills, but no country adopted this or any other boycott as a national policy. Just as a blockade against an enemy country may be an important part of ordinary warfare, so economic sanctions could be a highly effective part of ANAVET national defense but they need not be considered a necessity.

Much of the value of sanctions in both violent and nonviolent warfare can be psychological. Whereas many civilians of Axis X might hear of condemnations by other countries, the latter's *actions* would lend emphasis. Just as many U.S. citizens, relying on TV and newspapers for information, were unaware that their nation was condemned by the UN for invading both Grenada and Nicaragua, so many in Axis X, indifferent to news beyond censorship, might become more aware of international disapproval when they discovered there were shortages of needed consumer goods.

Meanwhile, in Manhattan the top brass might decide not to go much farther uptown than 46th and 47th Streets, the location of two major banks and no longer aim at 79th. Even before East River Park their colonels would report finding only stacks of gold bricks in the cut-open vaults of the Federal Reserve Bank and the U.S. Assay Office near Battery Park, and that Geiger counters showed no hints of radioactivity. In their headquarters aboard the *QE2* the generals would probably call Axis leaders for instructions. Should they wait for more gas to get to more bank vaults?

They would know that in the four ships' brigs there were now returned soldiers who had refused orders to do more clubbing, jabbing, or gassing of civilians who might cry out in pain but never in hate. That not only the prisoners were asking the question, "If the enemy had any nukes why didn't it use them to hit our ships instead of using civilians?" That in the two waterfront camps deserters were swimming away — that camp rolls of razor wire were now more for keeping soldiers in than civilians out. Finally the brass would know enemy propaganda was continuing without letup via planes, kites, rafts, banners, and PA systems, with almost daily innovations. They might add at the end of their request, "Troop morale low."

Let us suppose the Axis leaders' reply is to transfer all gold blocks to the ships "for detection by more sophisticated lab equipment here for traces of tritium activity." They may have already announced the main part of the "Intervention for World Peace," the incursion into Fort Knox. The limited supply of gas would be conserved for this, and for now New York would get no more. But while the new venture would get the tear gas, it would get few long-range planes, with too many still required to keep the disillusioned troops supplied with food. Leaders would scrap plans for doing Knox entirely by air — that is, parachutists building a long runway for big planes to land big guns for blasting open the actual fort housing the vault.

Rather, the leaders would decide to use tanks with 80 mm guns. They would ignore military advisors who favored asking the UN to request the U.S. to open the vault for international inspection in the same way that a U.S. president once ignored some generals' advice against invading Iraq. But the leaders would know the dramatic concept of Axis tanks forging their way through Kentucky to blast the citadel of tritium would well serve to divert attention of Axis X's citizenry, increasingly agitated about shortages and about reports of international condemnation and brutal attacks on unarmed New Yorkers. For readers, it will serve to show how ANAVET could resist a different weapon in a different rural setting of open highways.

7

Historical Accounts of Unarmed Resistance

Before proceeding with this new invasion, let us depart from the scenario to look at some actual invasions and/or occupations which were resisted by unarmed citizens who practiced, in various degrees, some sort of nonviolent actions. This will give the reader an opportunity to see how a fanciful account taking place in the year 2010 stacks up against real history.

India vs. Britain

The Indian non-cooperation with the occupying British which began in 1930 is the purest form of satyagraha resistance by a subjugated people on record. There had been much Indian violence over previous centuries, such as the notorious "Black Hole of Calcutta" in 1756 when 123 helpless English citizens were asphyxiated in a closed room. But the 1921–22 all-India non-cooperation struggle awakened the colony to the possibilities of unarmed struggle.

Early in 1930, Gandhi urged Lord Irwin, India's Viceroy, to meet to discuss Dominion status. Among the many injustices of British rule, Gandhi elaborated on the repressive Salt Laws, the colonial government's tax on Indian salt. He closed his letter by saying that if the meeting was refused, he and co-workers on March 11 would "disregard the provisions of the Salt Laws." Irwin did not reply. All of India waited excitedly. On March 12, with seventy-eight followers — whose names were published for the benefit of the police — Gandhi began the "March to the Sea." With much of the world watching, Gandhi and his followers walked for twenty-eight days, through hundreds of small villages in which many local leaders resigned their government positions and residents joined the procession.

When the marchers reached the sea at Dandi on April 5 after walking 241 miles, their numbers had grown to several thousand. The next day Gandhi picked up some salt left by waves on the hot Indian sand, thus breaking the law against possessing salt not bought from the government salt monopoly. The symbolic act signaled widespread violation of the Laws. People boiled sea water, and the Indian National Congress evaporated pans on Bombay roofs. Contraband salt was sold openly. Over sixty thousand Indians were kicked, beaten, and/or arrested, but none retaliated. Satyagraha being successful, Gandhi then announced he would raid the Dharsana Salt Works 150 miles up the coast from Bombay. He was arrested while sleeping in a tent but some twenty-five hundred volunteers marched without him to the Salt Works which was guarded by four hundred Surat (local Indian) police commanded by six British officers. Webb Miller, correspondent for United Press, described what happened:

> Dharasana Camp, Surat District, Bombay Presidency, May 22 (by mail). Amazing scenes were witnessed yesterday when more than 2,500 Gandhi "volunteers" advanced against the salt pans here in defiance of police regulations.
>
> The official government version of the raid, issued today, stated that "from Congress sources it is estimated 170 sustained injuries, but only three or four were seriously hurt."
>
> About noon yesterday I visited the temporary hospital in the Congress camp and counted more than two hundred injured lying in rows on the ground. I verified by personal observation that they were suffering injuries. Today even the British owned newspapers give the total number at 320. . . .
>
> The scene at Dharasana during the raid was astonishing and baffling to the Western mind accustomed to see violence met by violence, to expect a blow to be returned and a fight result. During the morning I saw and heard hundreds of blows inflicted by the police, but saw not a single blow returned by the volunteers. So far as I could observe the volunteers implicitly obeyed Gandhi's creed of non-violence. In no case did I see a volunteer even raise an arm to deflect the blows from lathis. There were no outcries from the

beaten Swarajists, only groans after they had submitted to their beating.

Obviously it was the purpose of the volunteers to force the police to beat them. The police were placed in a difficult position by the refusal to disperse and the action of volunteers in continually pressing closer to the salt pans.

Many times I saw the police vainly threaten the advancing volunteers with upraised lathis. Upon their determined refusal to recede the lathis would fall upon the unresisting body, the volunteer would fall back bleeding or bruised and be carried away on a stretcher. Waiting volunteers, on the outskirts of the pans, often rushed and congratulated the beaten volunteer as he was carried off the field. It was apparent that most of the injured gloried in their injuries. One leader was heard to say, "These men have done a great work for India today. They are martyrs to the cause."

Much of the time the stolid native Surat police seemed reluctant to strike. It was noticeable that when the officers were occupied on other parts of the line the police slackened, only to resume threatening and beating when the officers appeared again. I saw many instances of the volunteers pleading with the police to join them.

At other times the police became angered, whereupon the beating would be done earnestly. During several of these incidents I saw the native police deliberately kick lying or sitting volunteers who refused to disperse. And I saw several instances where the police viciously jabbed sitting volunteers in the abdomen with the butt end of their lathi. . . .

Once I saw a native policeman in anger strike a half-submerged volunteer who had already been struck down into a ditch and was clinging to the edge of the bank. This incident caused great excitement among the volunteers who witnessed it.

My reaction to the scenes was of revulsion akin to the emotion one feels when seeing a dumb animal beaten — partly anger, partly humiliation. It was to the description of these reactions that the Bombay censorship authorities objected among other things.

In fairness to the authorities it must be emphasized that the Congress volunteers were breaking laws or attempting to break them, and that they repeatedly refused to disperse and attempted to pull down the entanglements with ropes, and that the volunteers seemed to glory in their injuries.

In eighteen years of reporting in twenty-two countries, during which I have witnessed innumerable civil disturbances, riots, street fights and rebellions, I have never witnessed such harrowing scenes as at Dharasana. The Western mind can grasp violence returned by

> violence, can understand a fight, but is, I found, perplexed and baffled by the sight of men advancing coldly and deliberately and submitting to beating without attempting defense. Sometimes the scenes were so painful that I had to turn away momentarily.
>
> One surprising feature was the discipline of the volunteers. It seemed they were thoroughly imbued with Gandhi's non-violence creed, and the leaders constantly stood in front of the ranks imploring them to remember that Gandhi's soul was with them.[1]

India's satyagraha campaign for freedom was now on its way. A month later, along Bombay's beautiful ocean front, another dispatch told of an illegal assembly singing illegal freedom songs and illegally carrying Swaraj (home rule) banners. The *Chicago Daily News* published this dispatch from Negley Farson, its special correspondent in India:

> Bombay, June 21. Heroic, bearded Sikhs, several with blood dripping from their mouths, refusing to move or even to draw their 'kirpans' [sacred swords] to defend themselves from the shower of lathi blows — Hindu women and girls dressed in orange robes of sacrifice, flinging themselves on the bridles of horses and imploring mounted police not to strike male Congress volunteers, as they were Hindus themselves — stretcher bearers waiting beside little islands of prostrate unflinching, immovable Satyagrahis, who had flung themselves on the ground grouped about their women upholding the flag of Swaraj.
>
> These were the scenes on the Maidan Esplanade, Bombay's splendid sea-front park, where the six-day deadlock between police and Mahatma Gandhi's followers has broken out in a bewildering brutal and stupid yet heroic spectacle.
>
> The scene opened at six o'clock outside the Esplanade. At the police station facing the park some hundreds of yellow turbaned blue-clad, bare-legged Mahratti policemen were leaning on their dreaded bamboo lathis under the command of a score of English police sergeants in topees and cotton drill.
>
> At 6:45, marching in good formation down the tree-lined pleasant boulevard, came the first detachment of volunteers. This was the ambulance unit, mostly boys and young doctors, dressed in khaki with Red Cross badges on their arms. They marched past the waiting police without a glance to the south side of the playing field, where they parked their ambulances and brought out their stretchers. It was like nurses and orderlies preparing an operating theater.

At 7:00 began to come processions of white-robed volunteers bearing red, green and white banners, singing "We will take Swaraj — India Our Motherland." At the head of each walked a tiny detachment of women and girls dressed in orange robes, many garlanded with jasmine. They marched steadily on past the policemen and actually lined up behind the stretchers. They waited there in a long front down the boulevard for the order to march on the field.

I shall not forget the scenes which followed. Darkfaced [sic] Mahratti policemen in their yellow turbans marched along in column led by English sergeants across the field toward the waiting crowd. As they neared it the police went faster and faster. The Hindus, who may be willing to die but dread physical pain, watched them approach with frightened eyes. Then the police broke into a charge.

Many Hindus at once ran, fleeing down the streets — but most stood stock still.

Crash! Whack! Whack! Whack! At last the crowd broke. Only the orange clad women were left standing beside the prostrate figures of crumpled men. Congress volunteer ambulances clanging bells, stretcher bearers running helter-skelter across the field. Whack! Whack! Whack!

A minute's lull and then, with flags flying another column of volunteers marched onto the vast green field. A column of Mahrattas marched to meet them. They clashed — a clash, a rattle, dull thuds, then the faint-hearted ran and again there was the spectacle of the green field dotted with a line of fallen bodies and again the same islands of orange clad Hindu women holding up the flags of Swaraj.

And here in the center of one of these islands sat a little knot of men, their heads bowed, submitting to a rain of lathi blows — refusing to move until on a stretcher and completely laid out. And there were stretchers within two feet of the suffering men, waiting for them.

Then came a band of fifty Sikhs — and a heroic scene. The Sikhs, as you know, are a fierce fighting brotherhood. As soon as he can raise one, every man wears a beard which he curls around a cord or ties to his ears. The Sikhs also wear their hair long like women and curl it in a topknot under their turbans. These Sikhs were Akalis of a fanatic religious sect. They wore the kirpan, or sacred sword.

With them were fifteen of their young girls and women. The women also wore sacred swords, and although dressed in orange saris like Hindu women, they wore little cotton trousers which reached to their tiny, sandaled feet. They were pretty girls and not

> so loud voiced and excited as the Hindu ladies. They simply smiled as if they liked danger — which they do.
>
> One of them had her little baby, which she wanted to hold up before the police to dare them to come on. She laughed at me when my remark was translated that it was terrible to drag a child into this.
>
> Coming from all districts as representatives of the fighting Punjab, these Sikhs swore they would not draw their kirpans to defend themselves, but they would not leave the field. They did not.
>
> "Never, never, never!" they cried, to the terrific delight of their Hindu brothers, in Swaraj. "We will never retreat. We will die, we will!" The police hesitated before hitting the Sikhs. They asked their women would they not please, please, leave the field.
>
> "No!" said the women, "We will die with our men."
>
> Mounted Indian policemen who had been galloping across the field, whacking heads indiscriminately, came to a stymie when they faced the little cluster of blue Akali turbans on the slender Sikh men.
>
> "The Sikhs are brave men — how can we hit them?" It was not fear, but respect.
>
> But the police, determined to try to clear the field, at last rushed around the Sikh women and began to hit the men. I stood within five feet of a Sikh leader as he took the lathi blows. He was a short, heavily muscled man.
>
> The blows came — he stood straight. His turban was knocked off. The long black hair was bared with the round topknot. He closed his eyes as the blows fell — until at last he swayed and fell to the ground.
>
> No other Sikhs had tried to shield him, but now, shouting their defiance, they wiped away the blood streaming from his mouth. Hysterical Hindus rushed to him, bearing cakes of ice to rub the contusions over his eyes. The Sikh gave me a smile — and stood for more.
>
> And then the police threw up their hands. "You can't go on hitting a blighter when he stands up to you like that."[2]

In this case the smile in no way hid the fact the victim was badly hurt. Even children were among the four hundred thousand in India trained in satyagraha. Boys, singing the prohibited freedom songs in public, would continue as they were being knocked down by the long lathis of the police. When the disabled were carried off by the girls acting as nurses, fresh volunteers took their places.

The 1930 campaign led to an invitation to Gandhi to attend a conference in London, which did not result in independence. He was later placed under house arrest when the Indian National Congress passed a "Quit India" resolution in 1942, and was not allowed to continue publishing his freedom newspaper, *Harijan*, until 1946. Independence came in 1947.

Germany vs. Belgium and France

In 1923, from January until September, unarmed German civilians refused to cooperate with occupying troops from Belgium and France. By the terms of the Versailles Treaty, Germany was militarily impotent. When it fell behind in reparations payments to those two nations, they sent in troops with commissions to enforce collection. The Germans considered the invasion by the forty-five thousand troops illegal under the treaty's terms, and chose to oppose it by refusing to obey orders from the occupation officers.

German negotiators for the coal industry refused to make deliveries, and were court-martialed. After their convictions and fines, they were hailed as heroes by the thousands gathered outside the trials. Owners and managers next were arrested for failure to produce the requisitioned coal and coke. Miners then went on strike and shut off some electricity. Labor unions hastily organized a wider resistance. They pointed out that the Belgians and French needed the cooperation of German civilians for profitable results, that if workers stopped producing and employers refused to fulfill orders, the military could not carry out its demands. (This was an interesting twist on Bertrand Russell's proposed non-cooperation in World War I which was to be *against* Germany, not *by* it.)

German civil servants joined in, refusing to obey the invaders' orders, and were fined, imprisoned, or banished to unoccupied areas of Germany. Police, refusing to salute army officers, were similarly banished, leaving the occupied Ruhr district without police protection. The Mayor of Oberhausen shut off electricity for the city's railroad station, as did each of his two successors after he was banished.

Transport workers refused to handle trains taking requisitioned coal and coke into France, and by June of 1923 only four hundred were working out of a total of 170,000 for the Rhineland zone. Strikers also removed nameplates, signal plans, and similar information. The few trains the occupation could manage to run were boycotted by German patrons. Operators refused to drive streetcars whenever soldiers boarded. The occupation, unable to force the Germans to provide transportation, retaliated by stopping all of it, impounding barges and rolling stock, and putting troops in stations.

Shopkeepers refused to sell to soldiers and occupation officials, and sometimes closed entirely when troops were off duty. German patrons left cafes and other public places when soldiers entered, practicing the shunning policy. Posters put up by occupation orders were torn down. Newspaper personnel, refusing to heed occupation directives, were punished. (In 1923, when few homes had radios and broadcasting was just beginning, newspapers were the chief means of keeping informed.)

The lack of an effective propaganda campaign by the resistance has been cited as one reason for its compromised results, in addition to Germany's precarious economy and astronomical inflation. There was also insufficient relief for the invaded area from the rest of Germany, for when the occupation retaliated further by shutting down all business, the lack of money for food became an immediate problem for masses of workers. But chiefly, the resistance failed in its overall objective because it broke down into violence.

In June, saboteurs blew up a railroad bridge, killing ten Belgian soldiers and wounding forty. Favorable world opinion declined. The Papal Nuncio — later Pius XII — protested to the German Chancellor about the violent sabotage. This degeneration of the resistance gave the invaders exactly the excuse they needed not only for severe reprisals but also for further economic deprivations. Probably most of the 141 German deaths were for sabotage, actual or attempted. Even so, for a campaign lasting from January until its German termination in September, this figure is ridiculously low compared to what it would have been for an armed resistance.

Whereas in an ideal Kingian/Gandhian nonviolent action the outcome would be a victory for both sides, in the Ruhr campaign there was none for either. Lacking from the ideal was the development of personal friendships with individual soldiers which could break fighting morale. The head of the occupation army, General Degoutte, admitted later, "You have no idea of the difficulties I had, nor of the opportunities you had of exploiting them."

Denmark vs. Germany

The unarmed resistance of the Danes by strikes and boycotts against Nazi invaders in World War II was mixed with underground violence and sabotage. Most opportunities to convert the usually polite occupation were lost, the Danes leaving public places when soldiers entered, and otherwise refusing to engage in personal conversations. This shunning was also King Christian's practice. On his daily ride on horseback, he shook hands with citizens but refused to return Nazi salutes. One story then circulating indicates his importance as a morale builder. When the Nazis hoisted a swastika over a public building, he ordered it taken down. The Nazis refused. He said a Danish soldier would do it. They said he would be shot. "I will be that soldier," he replied, and according to the story the flag came down. Another story is that when the Nazis ordered all Jews to wear a yellow star, the King, along with many other non-Jewish Danes, also wore the symbol.

Even if the Nazis were not "loved as persons" in true satyagraha fashion, they were influenced enough by the Danes to realize the bestiality of Nazi anti-Semitism. One German officer leaked warnings to civilians helping Jews escape to Sweden. Of seven thousand ordered arrested, only 472 were captured.

German censorship in occupied Denmark was nullified by 538 underground newspapers with a circulation in 1944 that was said to be in the millions. Danes were also kept informed of their own resistance activities through reports smuggled to Britain and broadcast back over the BBC.

Eight Danes were executed when they sabotaged two arms factories, the Germans having announced that penalty in addition to a ban on strikes and an evening curfew. During one strike, the Nazis fired wildly into a crowd, and a general strike followed. In a futile attempt to break the strike, the Germans cut off water, gas, and electricity. (Unlike our Manhattan scenario where the resistance does this.) Only after the Nazis agreed to withdraw all street patrols did the Danes end the work stoppage. Sabotage in most cases was limited to industry and communication, and away from violence against persons. Perhaps because of this, German reprisals were less severe than in some other occupied countries.

France vs. Germany

Nonviolent resistance against Nazi occupation in World War II was practiced in an unusually well-organized degree in southern France. In 1942, thirty students handed the visiting minister of education of the collaborationist Vichy French government a statement:

> Dear Sir: We have learned that in Paris Jews are herded into stadiums and then deported. . . . Even though such may be the law in northern France, we will not obey it if applied here in southern France. No matter what the government orders, we will hide Jews.[3]

This proclamation is unique in the history of satyagraha truthfulness — openly announcing an intention to hide those sought by the government. Hiding a hunted object involves not only secrecy, most forms of which would be acceptable in ANAVET, but also deception and lying, which are not. Words, as well as mere physical shielding, would necessarily be involved. The statement was a truthful advance notice of an intention to be less than truthful.

Andre Trocme, pastor of the students in the village of Le Chambon, later wrote in 1955:

> Several times I had the opportunity of explaining clearly to the Vichy authorities . . . that we were hiding Jews and why we were doing so — that the law of God was love, and that the Church could not break that law. . . . In several cases, after such talks, persecution slackened.[4]

Advance phone warnings of raids often enabled Jews to be taken from homes to hide in the nearby forest. In 1955, *Fellowship* magazine carried an extensive discussion of the question, "Would you lie to save a life?" Of course, with no other choice, almost anyone would. When I discussed this personally with Trocme he said that "God has not provided us with a blueprint" of what to do in every situation, that often he had to pray about right procedures. "But it so happened," he continued, "that in each case when Nazis came to my door, there were no Jews in my house." Although having been spared the necessity of lying himself, he defended the right to do so. He said the Nazi officer, not really anxious to arrest Jews, needed only to hear from residents there were none in the village so he could file his report to that effect. Trocme felt the officer was not really being deceived.

Norway vs. Germany

In June, 1940, Norway's army surrendered to Nazi Germany. But even during the occupation, some Norwegian military forces went underground and continued fighting in an organization known as *Milorg*. A simultaneous civilian resistance was carried on by *Sivorg*. Much of this was also underground, but the part open and above is a good example of nonviolent non-cooperation.

The first open resistance came from youth. When the Nazi occupation tried to control their athletic clubs, hundreds of thousands objected and ended all organized athletic activities for the whole five years of German control. When the Germans dissolved Parliament in 1940 and set up their own administration, forty-three organizations sent the commissioner a protest letter. Some signers were arrested, others threatened, and finally all forty-three groups were dissolved. Radio sets that could be found were confiscated, and an underground press became the most important source of resistance news. At that time much civilian resistance went underground.

Perhaps, as in Hungary, the greatest handicap to Norway's resistance was political division. When patriots wore tiny Norwegian flags in their lapels, Norwegian storm troopers tore off the lapels. They and other Nazi sympathizers comprised the occupation's government under Vidkun Quisling, appointed in 1942. His edicts, however, were fearlessly opposed by the school system. Every teacher was asked to sign an agreement to give instructions "in the new view of society," and to oppose all attempts to ridicule or oppose the occupation's government. The teachers' organization responded with a counter-declaration for its members to sign:

> In connection with the communication which has been received, I herewith declare that I shall remain faithful to my vocation as a teacher and to my conscience, and that on this basis I shall continue to follow such instructions for my work as are lawfully given by my superiors.[5]

Whenever the Quisling regime attempted to introduce its edicts it was answered by the counter-declaration, and sometimes by teachers' strikes. In 1941 the government took over the teachers' organization, and in 1942 it created a new one with the "necessary authority to punish offenders." In that same month of February more than ninety percent of the country's fourteen thousand teachers mailed in a second statement to the government:

> I cannot take part in the education of the youth of Norway along the lines stipulated [by the occupation's government], as this is against my conscience. According to the statement made by its leader, membership in the [new teacher's organization] involves an obligation to give education along such lines, and also makes other demands which directly violate the terms of my appointment, I find it necessary to announce that I cannot consider myself a member of the [new teacher's organization.][6]

When the occupation regime cut off teacher's salaries, they continued to teach. The regime then closed all primary and secondary schools for one month because of a "fuel shortage." Some two hundred thousand parents mailed in letters, with their full names and signatures, saying it was against their consciences to have their children participate in the new Nazi-oriented educational program.

Eleven hundred teachers were then arrested all over Norway. Some were sent to concentration camps, and five hundred were imprisoned on a ship having facilities for only ninety-six. In the camps they were given hard work, fatigue drills, and starvation diets in an effort to force them to change their minds. But in one such prison only thirty-two out of almost seven hundred agreed to withdraw their protests.

In less than two months, the Quisling government had to capitulate to the teachers. They were returned to their schools, and lest anyone doubt that they had in any manner been brainwashed, they issued a longer and more explicit declaration than either of their previous two, stating that they would teach their pupils to believe in and uphold truth and justice and not teach anything violating conscience. The occupation regime had to accept this final defeat, and aside from making a few arrests, left the new declaration unchallenged. In an angry speech in May, 1942, Quisling said: "You teachers have destroyed everything for me!" By November, the last four hundred teachers were released from prison.

Resistance in the schools was not the only example of Norwegian nonviolence during the Nazi occupation. Also notable was the action of the state church, whose bishops published fifty thousand copies of a letter condemning: (1) the violence of Quisling's storm troopers; (2) the imposition of a Nazi-oriented judicial system leading to the resignation of the Norwegian Supreme Court of Justice; and (3) the police requirement that confidences given pastors were no longer inviolable.

About half the copies of this letter were confiscated. When Dean Fjellbu of Trondheim refused to be excluded from his cathedral and was dismissed, all bishops resigned. They were followed by all the clergy, and from Easter of 1942 until the war's end, Norway had no state church.

Most of these pastors, however, continued to perform their regular legitimate functions even without salary as long as they were able, continuing to make statements against the Quisling government. Two died in prison camps and thirty-five remained there until the war ended. Others were deported or had their movements restricted.

Another form of resistance, helping Jews to escape, was presumably participated in by both *Milorg* and *Sivorg*. In that clandestine project, some nine hundred out of Norway's seventeen hundred Jews were smuggled into neutral Sweden. The high figure of 734 Jews shipped to Nazi death camps may reflect the amount of pro-Nazi, pro-Quisling sympathy in Norway, and the handicap under which both resistances — armed and nonviolent — were working.

Individual German soldiers were usually treated with cool hostility, but one of Norway's nonviolent resisters, Diderich Lund, later wrote:

> Our attitude towards the Germans was . . . on the one hand . . . hatred of the brutality and inhuman cruelty which the Gestapo constantly practiced and the soldiers defended . . . tempered, however, by our understanding that we had no right to hold the individual responsible for all the acts done. . . .
>
> Now and then I tried to speak in a friendly way to a German soldier, but we very soon came to the point where I had to tell him how I looked on the Nazi system and the dirty work he was engaged in. At that point the friendly discourse was at an end, and I was lucky if I was not reported to the Gestapo.[7]

Lund also pointed out that German soldiers were even more afraid of this Nazi secret police organization than were the Norwegians, and further that it was "obvious to everyone" that thousands of soldiers were opposed to what they had to do. The few who dared to resist were shot as traitors.

German Democratic Republic (East Germany) vs. USSR

The East German Revolt (or "uprising") of 1953 began as a building trades strike against high work quotas imposed by the eight-year-old Soviet occupation. Polish tanks crossed into East Germany to support Soviet soldiers already there suppressing the strike. Within a week the strike had spread simultaneously to a hundred and fifty towns and involved half the labor force of East Germany. On many occasions and often as a result of extended conversations, Communist-controlled German police were successfully urged by demonstrators to refuse fixing bayonets, to lay down their arms, to desert to the strikers' side.

Polish tanks were met at the border in friendly fashion. One Polish officer got out of his tank, saluted, and announced he would not fire on them. The Soviets then ordered the tanks to return to Communist Poland and sent in their own. These seemed to have crossed the border previously and were already in isolated Soviet encampments throughout East Germany. Unfortunately, some confrontations with the Soviets were more violent. When one officer atop his tank amiably tried to wave a crowd aside, he was met with a hail of stones. In Jena, crowds pushed street cars in front of the tanks. Accounts say demonstrators fled when the Soviets opened fire, but that this fire was into the air, and that the tanks moved very slowly into the crowd. Some women actually stopped tanks in true nonviolent resistance fashion by sitting down in rows in front of them. There are no reports of any training in advance for this type of action.

Soviet soldiers watched indifferently at the Brandenburg Gate as East Berliners hauled down the Red flag, and even when they destroyed a Soviet bookstore on Alexanderplatz. Two Soviet lieutenants deserted and joined what they thought would be a successful revolution. When the revolt failed, one escaped to West Berlin and the other was executed. Seventeen or eighteen (accounts vary) Soviet soldiers and officers were executed for refusing to obey orders to shoot civilians. Today a monument in Berlin-Zehlendorf stands to their memory. Thus, in spite of advance planning, language difficulties, and much antagonistic violence, civilians were able to convert some soldiers.

When first ordered out of their local bases, the Soviet troops had been told they were going to pick up enemy leaflets. When they faced people instead, they were told that American agents were inciting an East German revolt. German leaders did make definite attempts to avoid bloodshed, locking up or destroying any arms captured from policemen and guards. In Halle they urged a crowd of seventy thousand demonstrating strikers to remain calm when Soviet troops and tanks arrived. At first they did remain calm, but when many began to shout abuses and spit on army trucks, strike leaders told the assembly to go back to their factories but not to work. Soviet troops in charge of East Germany's largest chemical plant arrested leaders of a sit-down strike, but it continued for many weeks because the army was apparently unwilling to use violence.

Unfortunately, lack of firearms did not prevent demonstrators from beating a few German officials and informers to death, thus giving the Soviets an excuse to put down the revolt with their own preponderance of violence. With no advance planning of how to resist without weapons, strikers were haphazard in their violence. In the first few days of the uprising, some observers assumed that well-oiled organizing must have been behind the almost simultaneous strikes, but apparently these were spontaneous. After this first lightning success — strikers came close to controlling all of East Germany — there was no uniform plan. There was no campaign strategy, no anticipation of the next step after the Soviet army entered the struggle.

A secondary reason for the revolt's failure was lack of support from the United States and Western Europe. No help came from West German radio stations similar to that which the invaded Danes and Norwegians had from the BBC in World War II. Allied authorities in West Germany actually blocked a broadcast calling for a general strike! In West Berlin they blocked a broadcast in Russian to the occupation troops by the Mayor. When a Russian refugee group in West Germany wanted to go to the border with a sound truck to urge occupation troops to refrain from using violence, permission was denied.

The Allies withheld support for the uprising because it was to their advantage politically to show the falsity of the Communist claim that western agitators were responsible for the strike. Historians have shown that the guiding Allied policy at this time was not to antagonize the USSR, their chief concern seeming to be the reunification of the two Germanies. The U.S. and the UN were already in a hot war with Communist forces of North Korea. Had the East Germans been able to show that theirs was a determined campaign to free themselves from Soviet domination with all the disciplined satyagraha which had freed India from Britain, the West might have felt it was worth a showdown.[8]

Hungary vs. USSR

The Hungarian Revolt of 1956 began as a peaceful protest on October 26 when students mimeographed sixteen demands against the country's pro-Soviet government. One was for the removal of a huge statue of Stalin, another for the removal of all of the Soviet military — twenty thousand troops and six hundred tanks. This openness of the students suddenly activated and united other Hungarians who had been longing for freedom. That evening two to three hundred thousand workers, students, Hungarian soldiers in uniform and military academy cadets gathered in front of Parliament. Other demonstrators tore down a Stalin statue.

At the Radio Building, where the students were trying to broadcast their demands, the much-disliked government security police — a uniformed group of mostly Hungarians — first fired tear gas, then bullets, into a crowd. The demonstrators, with at least three dead, retreated, but Hungarian soldiers, called in as reinforcements, refused to shoot, with many even joining the crowd and giving out guns. These weapons and others seized from security police and munitions plants were then used by insurgents who called themselves "Freedom Fighters." They exchanged fire with the security police, and throughout the following week with Soviet soldiers.

The first Soviet tanks appeared in Budapest the next day, and their indiscriminate firing killed two civilians and one Hungarian soldier, all unarmed. Yet that same day and the next, civilians engaged in considerable fraternization with Soviet soldiers — even as elsewhere in the city Soviet troops were engaged in fierce combat with the Freedom Fighters.

On October 25, almost ignoring the gunfire, a new group of eight hundred demonstrators which included many white-collar workers, marched on Parliament with the students' sixteen demands. When fired on by Soviet tanks, they marched back to the hotel where they had assembled. Finding several tanks and troop carriers stationed there, they asked crews why Soviets were firing on peaceful demonstrators. An Associated Press correspondent reported that civilians and soldiers were "smiling uneasily." But there seemed to be the friendliness, openness and fearless initiative which characterizes nonviolent action at its best.

After an hour's discussion, one soldier said the people's demands were just and that all should go to Parliament together. Some demonstrators decorated tanks with Hungarian flags and climbed aboard and rode along with the marchers to demand that the repressive Stalinists be expelled from power! When the marchers and tanks arrived at Parliament there were already twenty to twenty-five thousand people — about half women and children — waiting to hear the Prime Minister. Then, according to one account, a security police officer gave threatening orders for the crowd to disperse. Unfortunately, many people cried back "Assassin!" and "Pig!" and "Down with security police!"

Irrespective of the accuracy of such reports, it is important here to point out the fine but important distinction between insulting people by calling them derogatory names and expressing anger at repression by demanding such things as "Down with security police!" The latter could be ANAVET policy; the former could not. Security police on surrounding roofs (possibly some Soviet soldiers were with them) seem to have panicked at the threatening shouts. Fearing the demonstrators might seize the nearby Communist Party Headquarters, they opened fire. Some witnesses said Soviet tanks on side streets, not part of the march, fired not only on civilians but also on their own "fraternizing" tanks. Between three and eight hundred civilians were killed.

The satyagraha action — in which Hungarians had no previous training, and whose disciplines they were not consciously carrying out — was now mostly ended. In the ensuing violence the Freedom Fighters took over, and for a few days were victorious. The security police were abolished and a Communist favorable to the insurgents, Imre Nagy, became Prime Minister. But up to one hundred and seventy-five thousand more Soviet troops, and some three thousand more vehicles, were sent in from Central Asia. According to a UN report, "It would seem that the Soviet authorities had more confidence in troops who had no opportunity to be affected by European associations . . " i.e., by friendly Hungarians who spoke forthrightly about their opposition.

By November 3 the insurgents had lost control, and by mid-December, Hungarian factories and mines, idle for almost two months, were operating again. Stationed in both were the new "unaffected" troops. Thus, partly because the nonviolent resistance broke down in verbal violence, partly because Freedom Fighters wanted an armed revolt, and partly because many Hungarians were already involved in the repressive regime, the "mixed" opposition to Soviet control came to an end.

Czechoslovakia vs. USSR

David McReynolds of the War Resisters League, who was visiting Prague in 1968 when the motorized Soviet invasion began, filed an eyewitness account:

> Hand lettered posters went up everywhere. In Russian they urged the troops to leave. In Czech they urged no cooperation with the occupation and no cooperation with the collaborators. Every building sported signs. Cars had huge banners or posters tied to their

> fronts. . . . The Czechs were urging no armed resistance, no provocations, no cooperation, no collaboration. They were broadcasting in German, Polish, Russian, Bulgarian and Hungarian — special appeals to the troops to leave. . . .
>
> What was most impressive and most incredible was to see every tank, every troop carrier, every Soviet vehicle surrounded by Czechs who argued, climbed up on tanks and read manifestos, pleaded, explained, and in general tried directly to convert the army.[9]

Citizens had so much dialogue with the invaders, plus leafleting in Russian, Polish, and German, that on the third day soldiers were given counter-leaflets to answer the Czech arguments. On the fourth day of the invasion troops were withdrawn and replaced, while those who returned home were sent to isolated camps and not allowed to mix with the Soviet population. But the citizens learned in other ways that their troops had not been "invited." In Red Square five young Soviets held up signs protesting the aggression. One was Pavel Litvinov, a physics teacher who was the grandson of foreign minister Maxim Litvinov of World War II fame. Another of the five was a factory worker, reported to have said at his trial that the three minutes in the Square before arrest were worth the three years in prison.

The Czechs were not organized for non-cooperation; all such action, such as refusing to supply food and gasoline at an airport, seems to have been spontaneous. There was also some sniping and throwing of rocks and burning gasoline rags at tanks. Soviet troop rotation continued every two weeks. It was eight months before Soviet control was fully established. A violent resistance by such a nation so much weaker than its aggressor would have collapsed in a few days and there would have been far more fatalities than the fifty-five Czechs who died.

Monument in Zehlendorf, Berlin paying tribute to Soviet soldiers executed for refusing to fire on unarmed Germans in the 1953 labor strike against the East German government. Inscription reads: "To the Russian officers and soldiers who had to die because they refused to shoot at the freedom fighters of June 17, 1953." The number is put at seventeen, according to the Federal Ministry of All-German Affairs.

Photo by Till Bartels.

Buddhist monk blocks South Vietnamese government tank approaching Bho Da Pagoda in Da Nang, May 19, 1966.

UPI/Bettman Newsphotos.

Munitions ship USS *Sacramento* symbolically blockaded by small boats of "People's blockade" in Seattle, 1972.

Photo by Karen Engstrom. (courtesy Friends Journal.*)*

Munitions ship USS *Sacramento* is symbolically blockaded by small boats in Seattle, 1972. White sailor hat at right, three-quarters of the way down the side of the ship, is thrown in support of blockaders.

Photo by Karen Engstrom. (courtesy Friends Journal.*)*

"People's blockade" stops ammunition train outside Bangor, Washington Naval Ammunitions Depot, 1972. Twelve people were arrested, charged with trespassing and obstruction.

Photo by Karen Engstrom. (courtesy Friends Journal.*)*

Human blockade of toxic dump trucks, North Carolina, 1982. Fifty-five protesters were arrested. *Photo by Jenny Lebalme.*

Nuns leading prayers as the people face the Marcos loyalist soldiers in the Philippines, February, 1986.

Photo by Pete Reyes. Taken from People Power: The Philippine Revolution of 1986, *Monina Allarey Mercado, Ed.*

Filipinos, holding high a statue of the Virgin Mary, stand in the path of an armored personnel carrier.

Photo by Corazon Pasiona. Taken from People Power: The Philippine Revolution of 1986, *Monina Allarey Mercado, Ed.*

Filipino priest and a civilian face a tank sent to disperse the demonstrators.
Photo by Corazon Pasiona. Taken from People Power: The Philippine Revolution of 1986, *Monina Allarey Mercado, Ed.*

A single unarmed man blocks an approaching column of tanks in Beijing, June 4, 1989. *AP/Wide World Photos.*

Beijing students committed to a nonviolent march link arms to keep onlookers from joining.

(courtesy Ming Pao Publications Ltd., Hong Kong.)

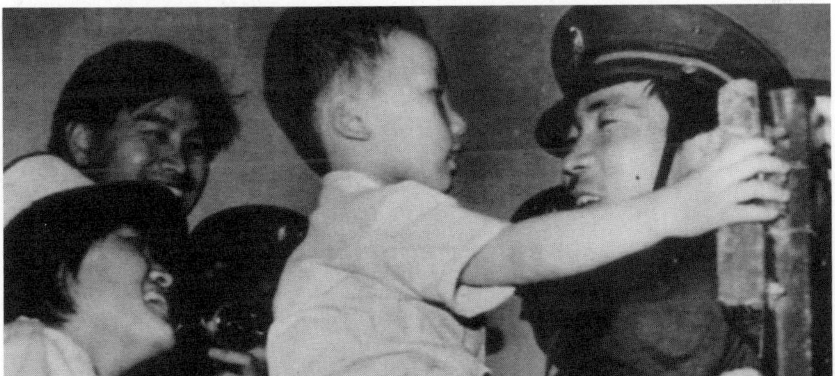

Beijing civilians blocking advance of army truck fraternize with one of its soldiers.

(courtesy Ming Pao Publications Ltd., Hong Kong.)

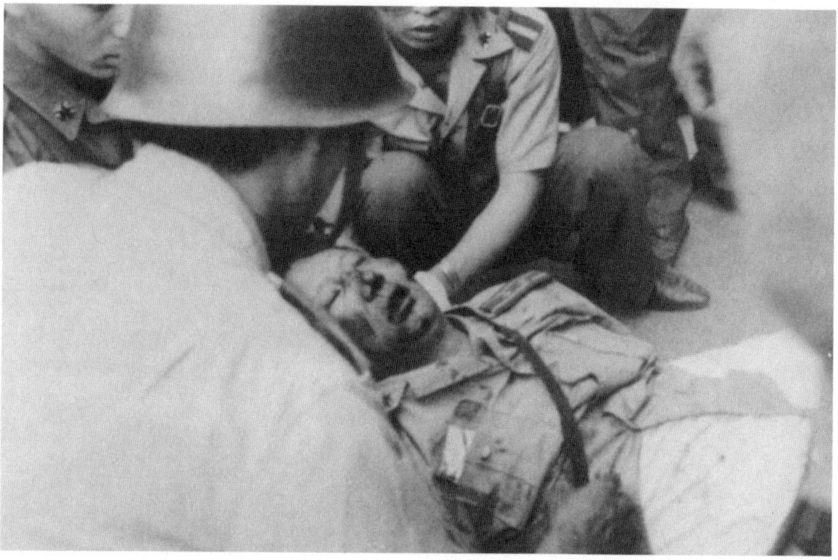

The Chinese government justifies its violence. Top: "Rioters" burn over a hundred military vehicles. Bottom: People's Liberation Army personnel wounded by "rioters."

Photos from "The June Turbulence in Beijing" circulated by Embassy of People's Republic of China, Washington, D.C.

A man places a bag of food on a Soviet armored personnel carrier flying the flag of pre-revolutionary Russia. Moscow, August 20, 1991.
AP/Wide World Photos.

Civilians block tanks in Moscow in August 1991. *Photo by M. Metzel.*

8
Scenario: Invaders Plan Capture of Fort Knox

After looking back into histories of invaded countries which used varying degrees of Gandhian/Kingian actions against aggressors, the reader can make comparisons between actual fact and imaginative future. Some of those examples involved tanks, which will be featured in the 2010 scenario to which we now return.

In Washington D.C., the Department of ANAVET National Defense's satellite pictures of Axis X seaports would show a tank division being loaded on cargo ships and converted oil tankers. Possibly even faces of generals in command might be recognizable, although this is in no way important for this scenario. Here, however, some readers might object, saying that in the Iraq War, U.S. satellites could not distinguish between a plywood tank and a real one. But the air over most seaports is not plagued with light-refracting layers of sizzling deserts, and these loading areas would not have ravines in which tanks could be hidden whenever a satellite passed over on regular schedule. Also, in our 2010 scenario we are assuming more satellites and greater frequency.

Even were it possible for Axis X to destroy all satellites in outer space, movements of its tank-carrying ships on open oceans and their progress and inevitably their final destination would, as with the troopships approaching New York, become worldwide knowledge. Let us say this destination is Newport News, with its excellent docking facilities for heavy equipment, the city also being the Virginia terminus of U.S.

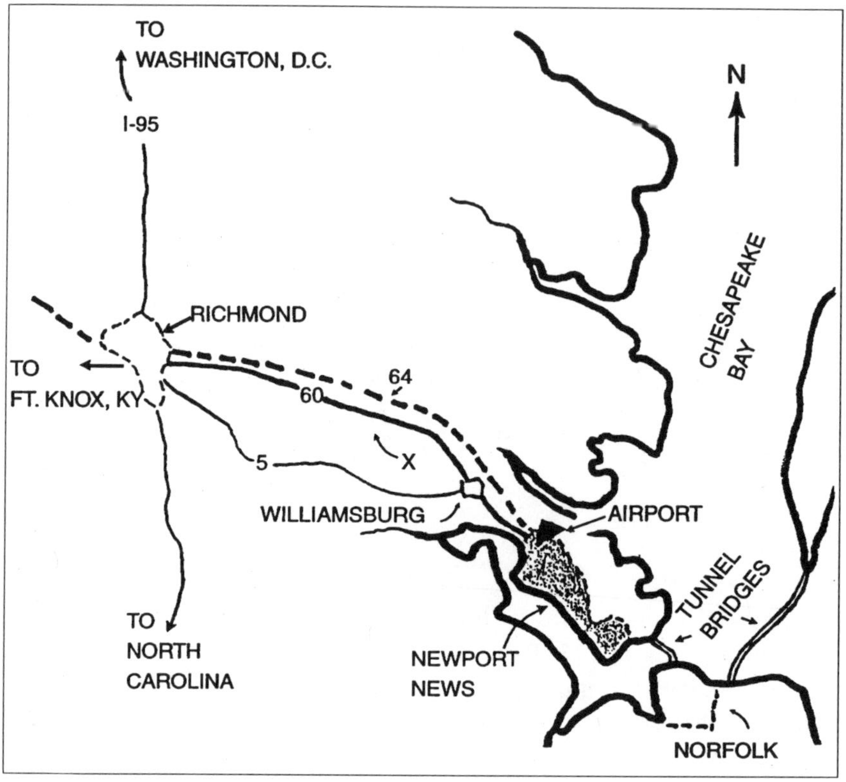

Figure D. Map of Eastern Virginia, showing occupied Newport News, Patrick Henry International Airport, and point X of resistance to tank advance on U.S. 60.

highway 60 leading to Fort Knox, Kentucky, 675 miles inland. (See Figure D.)

A first step in the civilian defense of the "Bullion Depository" — the vault — would be car-blocking the nearby landing strip of the former Fort Knox army base. But this would not prevent some two hundred paratroopers in round-trip planes from dropping near the vault, as happened at Manhattan power plants. To make a bad case for the resistance, let us assume Axis X planes can parachute enough soldiers, vehicles and supplies to quickly control the entire defunct base before resisters fully organize. Blockaders still rendering their cars inoperable would be helped to get outside the surrounding chain link fence. Former generals would advise that the invader's probable plan is for paratroopers to keep civilians away from the Depository until tanks arrive and can blast it open with 80 mm guns.

After the first landing of paratroopers the Depository's own civilian guards would be isolated in their living quarters inside, cut off from the outside except for communication. With their machine guns, a pistol range in the basement, ample supplies of ammunition, food, and their own water system — which, along with the strict "no visitor's" rule, were all components of the fortress-like Depository's security since its inception — they would be prepared for an extended siege. We are assuming that, except for the dismantling of the military base outside it, the Depository and its personnel have not yet been affected by the otherwise total disarmament in the U.S.

Let us suppose the tanks are aboard a convoy led by an Axis X battle cruiser. Arriving off Newport News it radios an ultimatum: "Surrender or be bombarded." Key provisions of the terms demand that the city cooperate in providing housing for officers and tank crews, meals and other provisions, tank fuel, repair facilities, exclusive use of the city's Patrick Henry International Airport and waterfront docks, stevedores to help unload motorized equipment, etc.

At a city hall meeting, the Secretary of ANAVET Defense would urge rejection and resistance, offering ten thousand trained ANAVET volunteers from Richmond, Virginia, to assist the city's nearly four thousand local ones. All resisters would try to prevent docking and unloading of tanks, and would assist in helping the wounded and fighting fires. The resistance would already have assembled a symbolic blockade, complete with waiting planes and sticky leaflets. Although similar to the one in New York, it would have fewer sailing craft and more fishing boats.

Here let us suppose that, as in some of the preceding examples, Virginians are sharply divided. The threat of shelling could arouse people in the nearby historic sites of Yorktown, Cape Henry Memorial, Jamestown Island, and restored Williamsburg. They would come to city hall in Newport News to plead that there be no bombardment of these national shrines.

Although the cruiser and armed oil tankers might shoot down news photographers' planes as defense against possible "bombing," Axis X ships could hardly use the same pretext for knocking out photographing by the UN Disarmament Verification Commission in its clearly-marked UN planes, or by its many satellites. Thus, unable to hide the damage the cruiser would be inflicting on non-military targets hundreds of miles away from the alleged weapons plant, it is doubtful if Axis X would so flout world opinion. Killing hundreds of thousands of unarmed civilians may be acceptable in ordinary military warfare, but here in Virginia even a score of mangled bodies would outrage TV viewers throughout the world. The "crusade to preserve world peace" would lose all credibility.

Perhaps many readers are not convinced by this reasoning. Let us assume that a majority at the city hall meeting are also skeptical. The Secretary of ANAVET Defense and the ANAVET resisters, after presenting such arguments, could not guarantee that the threat is empty. The cautious city council, pressured by frightened citizens, would then vote to surrender. It would declare Newport News an open city offering no resistance of any kind.

The disappointed Secretary and some resisters would leave to select some other location for resisting, out in open country, far from historic sites and worried inn keepers. Military advisors would have predicted the motorized division with the rubber cleats seen on its tracks was planning to travel on a paved highway, using it for the supply line of fuel, food, water, etc. for the 675 mile trip. It was likely that the simpler topography of U.S. 60 in Virginia would be seen as preferable to the vulnerabilities of the over/under passes of the more modern Interstate 64. It was also predicted that any tanks getting around a highway resistance would certainly try to return — that neither tanks nor crews would likely be prepared to crawl the full distance in lower gears, pushing down trees on the hilly and later mountainous terrain. Tracks would have to be refitted with steel cleats, and supply vehicles similarly tracked for such a rough, trail-blazing route.

Finally, advisors would suggest that while some resisters could also leave the highway to block alternate tank routes, it was more important that enough remain to block any tanks trying to return. The Secretary and his group would drive out on U.S. 60 and select a resistance point some eighteen miles west of Williamsburg. The nearest habitation would be a cafe half a mile farther west.

U.S. 60 at this site consists of two concrete lanes in each direction, separated by some eighty feet of a grassy center divider. Beyond the dirt aprons on both northern and southern sides are forests of scrub pines and oaks. The terrain has low, rolling hills, none steep. Car blockades being easily crushed and pushed aside, the resistance at the blue line — painted across both aprons and all between — would be human bodies.

Thousands of ANAVET-trained men and women would begin arriving in cars and buses from Richmond, Virginia, resistance headquarters thirty-three miles farther west. There an office of the Secretary of ANAVET Defense would be responsible for supervising the shuttling of resisters, arriving from all over the country, to the U.S. 60 boundary line, Here they would stay for shifts of two to five hours, sitting, standing, or lying on the concrete and divider. Richmond would be responsible for hot meals, extra blankets, folding chairs, supplementary rain gear and, in the city, medical care and sleeping quarters. The office would also have hundreds of potty booths and free phones installed at the edges of the woods.

Resisters would form in successive rows facing the blue line, and extending apron-to-apron. Each dozen or so would be an affinity group in the charge of its arm-banded monitor who would be responsible for seeing that members stayed within conduct agreed upon in ANAVET training — no liquor or drugs while on duty and, most important, no disrespect for persons during tense confrontations. At what times to lie prone, go limp, stand, advance, retreat, etc. would be the group's consensus decision and would be carried out under the monitor's direction. It would have been agreed that members unwilling to follow their monitor's orders would leave the group. Members would have gotten to know one another during the ride from Richmond and during their shift on the highway.

Rows would move progressively towards the front as earlier-arriving rows left for resting in Richmond. New arrivals would join at the rear of the fast-growing thousands, where the emptied cars and buses would load for return to the city. Reporters would be allowed on both aprons, and news helicopters would fly high or to the sides so as not to disturb resisters. Parked on one apron a hundred yards back of the line would be an ANAVET sound van with its two-way media connections. Most important, there would be translators to speak to tank crews if, as everyone nervously hoped, the tanks stopped.

Meanwhile, in Newport News all tanks would be unloaded with the enforced cooperation of its dock workers, and lined up on U.S. 60 (Warwick Boulevard) for the advance. Save for ships and tanks being covered with sticky leaflets, and Axis X helicopters upsetting a few catamarans, daytime docking would probably have been unresisted. However, let us assume that the night time unloading under floodlights may have tempted a few patriot-snipers, and that some soldiers were killed and wounded. Axis X would use the tragedy to reinforce its claims that the U.S. had never completely disarmed. Even were Newport News police successful in apprehending the "terrorists" according to surrender terms, this fact might not be mentioned in Axis X broadcasts to its soldiers in the field and its citizens back home. And, unfortunately for highway resisters, the attack would provide added combat incentive to tank crews. Bored after the long time at sea, they could now be itching for action to avenge their fallen comrades.

Resisters at "the front" would be receiving continuous news via the sound van and portable radios of the advancing tanks, such as: "Nineteen miles an hour . . . three columns using one westbound lane and both eastbound lanes . . . tanks, personnel carriers, trucks, and jeeps, totaling about 800. . . ." Some affinity groups might be singing "We Shall Not Be Moved." Others might be learning phrases in Axis X language:

"Hello."

"You are invading our highway."

"We belong here, not you."

"The U.S. has no weapons."

"Refuse orders to hurt unarmed civilians."

"Go home!"

Well before the first perceptible "OOM" of the distant roar of the approaching vehicles there might be a frightening pass of a low-level fighter jet, its sonic boom breaking windows in the cafe. All on the highway would watch the departing plane go into a steep climb, turn, and then come back at them in a faster-than-sound dive. Many, fearing a drone crash on the highway, would scatter to the sides. A second, much worse boom might literally sweep standees off their feet and knock down their posters. When there was quiet again the van, supposed to warn of all impending situations but having no notice of this one, would announce that both passes were scare tactics, and advise each group to have its own lookout for fast planes.

As soon as the first tanks were seen over a slight rise in the highway all resisters would sit facing them. The three columns, not slowing from their now twenty-one miles per hour on their "kloppeding" rubber-cleated tracks, would immediately start blowing all horns. Resisters would hold hands across entire rows and look straight ahead at the furious oncoming steel. The religious ones among the group would be praying. If all in an affinity group were from the same church or denomination they might do so in unison.

At this tense moment what would the highway resisters be feeling about the onslaught? A probable bloody massacre, or another scare tactic? In their ANAVET training to "negate all violence," actual or threatened, they would have studied historic examples of vulnerable bodies blocking vehicles. Trainees who had decided there was little chance a tank division would stop for a human blockade, probably would not have come. On the other hand, few of the ten thousand sitters would feel really sure the tanks would stop. Because of the mixed record of past vehicle-body confrontations, most would assume their lives were at risk.

Until the deliberate massacre in Beijing of June 4, 1989, there seem to have been no actual fatalities of nonviolent resisters run over by vehicles in the sixty-nine years since a historic confrontation in 1930. In this long period there were several instances of nonviolent blockaders being deliberately injured, but fortunately escaping death.

In 1930, during India's freedom campaign recounted earlier, Indian merchants were urged to join the consumer boycott against British cloth. Many pledged not to handle it, but one dealer continued to sell truckloads of Manchester cloth to small shops outside Bombay. Several months of picketing and appeals by leaders proved futile.

Finally a young campaigner, Bapu Gano, lay down on the company's driveway. An English driver specially hired for the task, drove a delivery truck over Gano, who died instantly. His martyrdom caused indignation in all of Bombay. The dealer joined the boycott, and the thoroughfare where the tragedy occurred was renamed Bapu Gano Road. During the rest of the "Quit India" campaign there seem to have been no reportable injuries to civilians blocking troop trains.

In my readings of peace literature since the mid-thirties, I found the next injury of a nonviolent blockader by a vehicle, which seems to have been at least partly deliberate, occurred in August 1957, in Wyoming. There, Kenneth Caulkins and others were trying to block trucks engaged in constructing a base for Inter-Continental Ballistic Missiles. In June the group, including Caulkins' wife Ellanor, had conducted a public opinion poll in nearby Cheyenne. After being ejected from the base while distributing leaflets, they sat in the road, not entirely blocking access. Drivers went around them, but when one came too close to Kenneth's hip, the group was arrested, and five were jailed. The protest continued through mid-September.

Civilian blocking of Soviet tanks in Jena, East Germany, has already been mentioned. Not mentioned in the Soviet tank invasion of Czechoslovakia in 1968 was an incident ANAVET trainees would have noted very carefully. At a bridge over the Upa River villagers blocked oncoming tanks with their bodies for *nine hours*, after which the tanks turned around and went home.

During the Vietnam war, students of the University of California at Berkeley sat in front of troop trains but were bodily thrown off the tracks by U.S. marshals ahead of the slowly moving locomotives. No serious injuries were reported. But in the same era possibly fatal ones were miraculously avoided in Oregon. The following account appeared in *Fellowship* magazine:

> Risking serious injury and/or arrest, People's Blockaders in the Portland area engaged in three separate blockade attempts in late October and early November to protest the accelerated shipment of arms to Indochina by the Nixon Administration.
>
> On October 28th, 35 blockaders from the AFSC-sponsored People's Blockade group caused a 118-car freight train to come to a complete stop in Vancouver, Wash. in order that they might inspect the train for possible ammunition cars (Bombs on such trains are carried daily through Vancouver on their way from Midwest munitions plants to the Bangor Naval Ammunition Depot from which they are shipped to Vietnam.) However, Burlington Northern Railroad officials ordered the train's engineer to proceed after the inspection had just begun while most of the group of blockaders were still seated on the tracks less than 25 yards from the train. As the train approached, one of the blockaders, Steve Adler, simply stood his ground in plain view of the engineer. Steve was knocked to the ground between the tracks by the huge locomotive and was completely covered by the front of the train before the engineer stopped the train. Fortunately, neither Steve nor other blockaders sitting or laying across the tracks was injured. Vancouver police moved in quickly clearing the tracks and arresting six of the blockaders who refused to move for trespassing.
>
> A week later, at the same site, Burlington Northern officials again forced a risky confrontation by ordering another train, whose 66th car was plainly marked as carrying ammunition, to proceed on tracks occupied by another blockade group. This time when the train reached the group, five of the blockaders grabbed hold of the front of the locomotive and were carried some 20 yards before the train was stopped. Again, no one was seriously injured, though one participant was taken from the scene by ambulance after having

> been thrown from a height of 10 feet by an over-zealous Vancouver police officer removing him from the train.
>
> Vowing to continue the train blockades, one participant explained, "So long as the ceasefire is not a reality for the Vietnamese people who are still being killed by these same bombs, there is no reason for us to engage in a ceasefire at home." [1]

News of any nonviolent blockading in Vietnam itself was barely alluded to in the peace movement, save for a notable photo of a lone Buddhist monk stopping a tank. But in the 1986 nonviolent overthrow of the Marcos regime in the Philippines, the civilian blocking of tanks was publicized by the new president herself, Corazon Aquino: "The world saw and recorded a people who knelt in the path of oncoming tanks and subdued with embraces of friendship the battle-hardened troops sent to disperse them." [2]

The first serious, deliberately-inflicted injury by a moving machine since Gano's death in 1930 seems to have been that suffered by Brian Willson on September 1, 1987. At the train gate of the Concord (CA) Naval Weapons Station both his legs were severed below the knee.

This munitions shipping station had been a focal point for many peace protesters in Vietnam days when it was handling napalm. Many blocked its driveway for incoming loaded trucks, one resister even chaining himself to one of them. Protesting was revived in 1987 at the station for its key role in shipping munitions to the Contras in Nicaragua. Willson, a Vietnam veteran, lay down with two other nonviolent protesters on the tracks of an incoming munitions train. Its crew had been given advance notice, and two standing demonstrators held a banner across the tracks. Some forty-five supporters stood close by. The train did not slow. Willson tried to jump off the tracks with the two others but was caught by wheels and dragged twenty-five feet. He lost both legs and suffered lacerations to his head, cheek, and ear.

After Gano in 1930, there seem to have been no deliberately-caused deaths to nonviolent blockaders until the massacre in Tiananmen Square in Beijing, China, on June 4, 1989. The number of fatalities, estimated by Amnesty International to have been thirteen hundred, may never be known, even by the Chinese government which caused them. That vast protest, with sometimes as many as 2.1 million people massed together, with hunger strikes and student demands ranging over several weeks, has far too many ramifications to offer the simple answers of previous examples to the question, how safe is a nonviolent blockader facing an oncoming vehicle?

After studying the valuable collection of statements by protesters themselves, government leaders on both sides, and reporters, and many photographs in the collection "June Four,"[3] I concluded that this was a complicated example of a nonviolent project breaking down, in this case because of an unmanageable influx of outside supporters.

After some clashes between police and protesters on April 22, students had organized a "Federation of All-Beijing College Students Unions (Interim)" and adopted peaceful methods. On April 27 some two hundred thousand students went through Tiananmen Gate, pushing past eighteen lines of uniformed policemen. Both sides exercised great restraint, and no clashes were reported. On the contrary, in true nonviolent style, students cheered the police, shaking hands and shouting "People's police have love of the people," and "We salute the police." Students were cheered by over one million people on both sides of the streets. But to prevent them from joining the procession and causing "unwanted incidents," marchers along each side innovatively linked arms.

After the fourteen-hour march, and with the continuing demands of the students in Tiananmen Square, the movement spread. In Changsha, provincial capital of Hunan, over six thousand students marched with one thousand workers while police with electric clubs looked on. This was the first time workers joined students.

On May 20, as the two hundred thousand students in Tiananmen Square were supporting a hunger strike in protest to his speech, the Premier declared martial law. All demonstrations and any news reporting of them were banned. Ignoring the new restrictions, citizens used their bodies to stop four thousand troops arriving in trucks and buses. At another location they surrounded helmeted troops in thirty trucks. The soldiers reportedly had not been allowed to get any news of the month-long peaceful demonstration except an official government statement about "turmoil."

That day of May 20 saw even trains being stopped elsewhere with no violence. The day seemed a good example of satyagraha, yet the Premier spoke of "cases of beating, smashing and looting," the first such allegation, and apparently unconfirmed. The next day, twenty thousand workers and students from outside Beijing formed a corps to protect students in the Square. This acceptance by the committed students of so many presumably untrained in self-restraint now appears to have been a mistake. Better the previous linking of arms to keep out the uncommitted. Students were reminded by their leaders not to strike back if beaten, but that day there were clashes, one in which forty civilians and, unfortunately, one soldier were injured.

At this point we cannot rule out deliberate governmental provocation. The forces of massive and superior violence, unable for several weeks to conquer those who have renounced violence, would seek to change the confrontation into one of violence vs. violence, an arena where superior violence can win. With no reporters allowed, the army could easily escalate the injury of even one soldier into a major battle. The temptation in the Square to provoke violence, as an excuse to quell it by violence, would have been great.

The next day, May 22, there were more troop clashes with civilians, and in a Beijing suburb several dozen students were injured by bricks and beltings. On June 2, just before the massacre, some soldiers gave guns to nearby students and others, who were suspicious and wisely turned them over to the police and got receipts. Some civilians did retaliate against brutalities by calling the soldiers names and throwing stones and bottles but there were no deaths until June 3, when a speeding army car killed three.

The government's strategy here was to use fresh troops unfamiliar with the previous troop's fraternization with demonstrators. The tactic is reminiscent of Soviets using fresh tanks and crews to replace those withdrawn from Prague who had been engaged in discussions with Russian-speaking Czechs. The new replacement Chinese troops on June 3 began forcing their way into the crowded Square, provoking incidents to incite violence. At one gate they used clubs and tear gas, but people blocked entry for some three hours. Then some in the crowd threw rocks at soldiers. The satyagraha of the well-organized students, so patiently and faithfully practiced by them for so many weeks in Tiananmen Square, finally broke down.

In the melee that followed, soldiers as well as civilians were injured. The angry crowd overturned an army jeep and broke windows in a bus carrying weapons. Presumably, troops at this point had only clubs. The government warned that martial law was in effect and that *any means necessary* would be used to enforce the order to clear the Square. Unfortunately most students still living there in their tents believed the earlier promise that the army would never hurt them.

Late on the night of June 3 soldiers in the Square, which still had several hundred thousand students, workers, and others, began shooting and killing. At 12:04 A.M. on June 4 the first speeding armored car arrived, followed by some ten thousand troops. People who bodily tried to block the car barely escaped, but they were able to force a collision between the next two, injuring many soldiers and killing one. Soldiers fired into the air until 2 A.M., then fired hollow point bullets at everyone. Tanks followed. The TV news picture of a lone civilian standing in front of a line of them was seen worldwide. When the tanks attempted to pass him, he moved sideways. He climbed up on the tank and spoke to the soldiers, then again stood in front of the stopped tanks. They moved ahead after he was pulled out of their path by people fearing for his life. But the tanks rolled over any other resisters as well as the exhausted students in tents. By daylight, as ambulances and trucks hurriedly gathered up the casualties, the massacre was almost over. Some estimates of the dead range many times higher than the thirteen hundred mentioned by Amnesty International.

Of major interest to ANAVET trainees studying the Beijing tank-involved atrocity would be the government's immediate denials and attempts to hide the evidence, and its later excuses when it could no longer ignore such. Its official report of June 6 gives the following figures, with the proviso that "these statistics may change as more information (becomes) available":

Officers and soldiers wounded: 3,000

Civilians wounded: 2,000

Civilians and soldiers killed: 300

Students killed: 23

The government's June 6 booklet contains page after page describing civilian brutalities against the army. Major General Shao Songgao is quoted as being in his jeep June 3 when "A young man came out from the crowd of a sea of pedestrians. He pulled my hair and slapped my face. The young man then shouted, 'They came here to suppress the people. Beat him.'" Songgao goes on to say some in the crowd used their fists, and that when passing doctors were taking him to the hospital some civilians helping were also beaten by the crowd. (The "young man" sounds much like some provocateurs who infiltrated committee meetings of peace activists during the Vietnam era.)

Official government photos of troop buses and armored cars on fire are shown to prove government claims that 364 army vehicles were burned. Some of the soldiers reportedly "cruelly beaten" to death, one or two said to be mutilated, were reported to have been burned up with gasoline. Nothing in these accounts hints that many of the civilian corpses were also burned by the army and the ashes hastily carried away to hide evidence, or that blood on the pavement was washed away before reporters were readmitted to the Square. Nor was there any hint of the students earlier offering food to soldiers and engaging them in conversation.

The evidence indicates the army was the first to kill, and that unfortunately civilians retaliated in kind — although to a very limited extent. Students were overconfident of army promises of immunity, and many might have saved their lives even by openly facing tank drivers instead of being crushed to death out of sight in their tents.

In Moscow in August 1991 the attempted military coup by right-wing Soviets stands as an excellent example of nonviolent resisters confronting tanks. Unlike Beijing, this resistance was more spontaneous than planned; like Beijing, no foreign power was involved. Yet there were some language differences. A Russian news reporter, Alexander Pronozin gives an overview:

> The coup leaders immediately took control of the mass media, using it to give legitimacy to what they had done . . . (and) drew up a plan to storm the White House [parliament building] and kill Yeltsin and 11 other senior Russian leaders. A special section of the 'KGB Department of the Struggle Against Terrorism'. . . was given responsibility . . . but when it became clear to them that they would have to kill hundreds or thousands of unarmed civilians, the entire subdivision refused to carry out the order despite the danger to themselves. Thus the weapon of nonviolent resistance appeared not only within the public but within the armed forces.
>
> Units which had been persuaded by the population not to engage in repression were taken out and replaced with fresh arrivals.
>
> Protesters who spoke the languages of non-Russian nationalities were selected in order to appeal to soldiers in their native tongue.[4]

Most readers will remember the picture of Boris Yeltsin, Russia's leader during President Gorbachev's house arrest, speaking to a crowd of civilians and soldiers from atop a personnel carrier. In good ANAVET fashion he called for civil disobedience, strikes, and no violence. Perhaps he remembered how USSR tanks had been confronted by unarmed Czechs back in 1968. Certainly he and all Russian leaders well knew that civilians in both Azerbaijan and Lithuania had faced up to Soviet tanks as recently as the preceding January.

David Hartsough, Executive Director of Peaceworkers (San Francisco), was invited to Moscow after the coup to give training in nonviolent civilian-based defense. He tells of the importance of ordinary people in defeating the coup:

> Many say Boris Yeltsin was the key figure in the overthrow of the August coup in Moscow . . . As a result of discussions with many Russian citizens . . . I believe that the tens of thousands of courageous Russian citizens — who risked their lives standing up for their beliefs in democracy, freedom and human dignity and nonviolently resisting and non-cooperating with illegitimate authority — are the ones who defeated the coup.
>
> Imagine, if you can, waking up the morning of August 19 and seeing thousands of Soviet tanks occupying Moscow.
>
> Thousands of people all over Moscow gathered their courage and went out into the streets, surrounded the tanks, greeted the soldiers with cakes and cigarettes and roses, and entered into dialogue with them. People knocked on the tanks and said to the soldiers, "Why are you here? Who gave you orders to bring these tanks into Moscow? Are you going to shoot at people? Whom are you going to shoot?"
>
> People built physical barricades of trolley cars, buses, old pieces of metal and box springs around the White House, not so much because that would stop the tanks more than a few minutes, but to enable them to enter into dialogue with the soldiers about what they were doing, and to convince them to discontinue the attack.
>
> The women at the barricades kept encouraging everyone to "keep nonviolent. Don't hurt the soldiers." . . . The official policy . . . was to strongly discourage any violence to the soldiers and to try to win them over.
>
> When the Parliament members heard of the impending attack some of them traveled to the edge of Moscow and met with the KGB troops. When the troops heard they would have to kill hundreds or even thousands of civilians to fulfill their mission, they refused orders to carry out the attack.
>
> Multitudes of people refused to obey the curfew on the crucial night of August 20-21. Public transit continued to run. It felt as if most of Moscow was on the streets. This mass disobedience was a tremendous psychological blow to the coup leaders.
>
> People throughout the society, including elected officials, soldiers, KGB officials, Communist Party leaders, students, transportation workers, and journalists, decided to listen to their consciences and their sense of what was right and just. . . .
>
> The coup leaders had at their disposal more than four million soldiers, hundreds of thousands of tanks, sophisticated military

> aircraft and nuclear weapons. The world's second most powerful military state was overcome by a people armed with their courage and conviction . . . (not) frightened into submission by threats of death or imprisonment.[5]

Hartsough also mentions that resisters organized themselves into groups of 100 to maintain discipline and to keep their spirits up, a counterpart of the smaller "affinity groups" in our scenario.

Capt. Michael Golovko, a Soviet military journalist with two decades of Navy service, tells how he was run over by an armored personnel carrier which was advancing on the White House in his *A Chronicle of a Night on the Barricades*:

> The first words should describe the tracer bursts of machine-gun fire striking through the grayish-black sky, the grinding sound of trolley buses smashed by the military equipment, the shouts of unarmed people rushing to stop the Armored Personnel Carriers . . . I was among these people at the barricades on the night of August 20–21.
>
> There are many youths with bags and knapsacks. They look at my Navy uniform, waterproof cape, and captain's chevrons cautiously: "Are you with us? Will you be punished for being here? Do you think they will shoot?"
>
> 12:38 a.m.: "The assault has begun! Equipment is moving along the Sadovoye. Anyone who is free, go to the defense of the barricades!" I run with the others . . . I reached the barricade of trolley buses . . . close to Smolenskaya Square. . . . A few tipsy characters loitering nearby ran away the moment the APCs appeared. Those who stayed there understood completely what was going on and what might happen. They were ready to stand till the end and to lie down under the tank treads.
>
> I thought that the APCs would not crush me right now in my uniform of a senior military officer which was clearly visible in the light of their headlamps. They would listen to me, at least. Or simply arrest me, and the fuss would make a break [delay]. And so I stepped forwards, in front of the oncoming APC.
>
> But I was mistaken. The carrier stopped for a moment, half a meter in front of me, staggered, and then went fast ahead and pressed me down under the platform-type frame. Quite by lucky chance I was directly between the treads and got off with nothing more than bruises. I was pulled out from under the treads of the second moving APC.
>
> In the midst of people who were shouting and moving around, the first and second APC started crushing the barricade. After one or

two of those who were riding atop the APCs were knocked off and by a miracle remained alive, I decided I should stop these APCs by all means. I covered the vision slit of the first carrier with my waterproof cape. It stopped. The remaining [7 or 8] APCs stood still and did not seem aggressive. The carrier drivers appeared up to the waist and squabbled with the defenders.

After taking the blow from the APC there was a buzzing in my head, and my knees and left hand were aching. Someone helped me to reach the wall of a house. While sitting on the pavement I saw young fellows climb on the armor of a tank and spread the tarpaulin which had been rolled up behind the turret. I saw them falling, knocked down by a fast rotating barrel. I saw people shove iron posts into the tracks to try to stop the APC, and how the posts were dragged by the tracks, tearing off some minor units [parts].

A strange man standing not far from me tries to persuade people to stop the senseless, in his opinion, resistance . . . Nobody pays attention to him. After some rest I join the living ring of people surrounding the White House.

1:22 a.m.: That part of the chain of people where I am standing is under the command of a shortish, black-haired man. The essence of his instructions: in case the military equipment arrives, let it go through; try to convince the soldiers not to use force against the population; don't insult them; don't throw sticks and stones; no bottles of gasoline; only civil disobedience and appeals to support the legal government.

1:40 a.m.: Far off the sound of heavy equipment is heard. Everyone steels themselves, joins hands tighter, closes in. But the sound passes by and vanishes behind dwellings. Somebody cries out "Hooray!" A bottle with gasoline and a hunting knife are taken away from someone in the cordon and another order is given to hand in such weapons.

2:27 a.m.: People have begun walking around. Defenders of the White House are grouped around the tanks which came over to the Russian Government. Women, who did not leave despite all encouragement, give us hot coffee. . . .

Some people who came from Kalinin Avenue say that . . . beside the two that died under the APCs, a soldier was shot by an officer, and there were three other victims. I hope that the information is not a complete truth.

5:39 a.m.: Little by little people disperse. . . . Another night seems to be a victory.

TV news showed one civilian lying in front of an advancing tank, then getting up as it came too close. Final reports list only three

> fatalities for the entire two day confrontation, all unarmed civilians trying to stop APCs.[6]

Dmitri Komar, twenty-three-year-old veteran of the Afghanistan war, jumped onto APC #536 and tried to blind it with its tarpaulin. Thrown off, he jumped into the open hatch. The vehicle lurched and he was thrown out end dragged alongside. His friend Vladimir Usov, a thirty-seven-year-old former naval officer and son of an admiral, was shot while running to help him. Igor Krichevskii, Jewish architect and poet, threw a stone at the APC and was shot while moving towards it (the vehicle later set on fire by a Molotov cocktail). Four others were wounded by gunfire.

What are the lessons for the resisters on U.S. 60 of these tragedies in Russia and China?

9

Scenario: Tanks Employ Scare Tactics

In our hypothetical confrontation on U.S. 60 the trained resisters would have studied, or at least would be familiar with, the blockading stories in the previous chapter. They would know their lives were at risk with the oncoming tanks, but they might have learned how to reduce those risks. One lesson from the Russian coup could be that the brave Komar, in jumping into an open hatch, may have retained too much of his military training and acted too quickly, with too much surprise. His action might have been considered heroism in ordinary violent warfare, but not in a case when one should not frighten an adversary. It is easy to see how the APC crew, trained to act quickly, and possibly not knowing he was the same person who merely had tried merely to obstruct their vision, might have feared that he carried a grenade so did not wait to learn his nonviolent intentions. In any case, U.S. 60 resisters with their open and slower motions would try to avoid such misapprehensions.

The example of the massacre at Tiananmen Square, while sobering, would not be intimidating, there being too many factors favoring U.S. 60 blockaders. First, as in Moscow, they would have the open worldwide media coverage which tends to inhibit military atrocities. Overhead there would be even more, for a totally disarmed U.S. would have an extensive spy satellite system, covering not so much the territory of possible invading nations as that of its own defended fifty states. It would invite other nations and the UN to monitor and report to the world all details of ANAVET resistance against tanks. Had military satellites of the U.S., and possibly USSR, which can see at night and through clouds, been trained on Tiananmen Square in 1989, they could have recorded the number of casualties on the open pavement quite accurately, and even caught individual acts of violence. But no such information would then have been released lest it reveal military capabilities of intelligence gathering.

The major factor favoring U.S. 60 resisters would be their advance training and organizing. Small affinity groups, each with a monitor in charge, would be far more manageable than was possible in the Square. Supporters along the sides of Highway 60 might number in the thousands, not millions, and none would be allowed to "defend" the trained resisters. The latter, when weary, would not be sleeping on the highway but resting in Richmond, replaced by fresher ANAVET volunteers from rows behind. Satyagraha on the highway would have a far better chance of not breaking down, either by well-intentioned outsiders or by provocateurs.

We shall assume this discipline holds, that there are no snipers in the woods, that not one rock or bottle is thrown over the heads of supporters at the oncoming tanks, that all resisters remain sitting in place to show they have no intention of scattering. We also assume that by now every tank crew, every foot soldier in a carrier, would be at least partially aware of the U.S.'s claim that it has no secret weapons and no military armed services. Their vehicles might still have some sticky leaflets, left from the showers dropped during unloading and deploying in Newport News. And before this, while still confined below deck, many would have seen banners through port holes.

Up until this actual point of contact with nonviolent resistance probably few of the ten thousand division's personnel would have lent much credence to the U.S.'s claims. But some of the more logical minds might wonder why, if there were some weapon, it had not been used by now. "The enemy could have blown us up at sea, while docking, or here on the open highway. All they have fired at us is a few sniper's bullets."

We here assume that the general in ultimate charge of the oncoming tanks, riding at the head of one of their three columns, has no intention of allowing civilians to block him from his Fort Knox objective. But he would also be aware of the presence of neutral international reporters and photographers everywhere, along the aprons, probably up in trees, and up in the air just below the blue-and-white UN observation planes of its Disarmament Verification Commission. And while all civilian aircraft were observing his orders to stay outside his airspace over the highway, which was reserved for his fighter jets and observation helicopters, there was no way he could now hide a massacre. Probably surprised that the civilians remained sitting as his horn-blaring tanks raced towards them, he would make the quick decision he had not planned for: to negotiate.

Assuming he remembered the world's condemnation of China for its Tiananmen Square massacre, he would also remember that even there the government negotiated, however unsatisfactorily, for weeks, before finally cracking down. Now, in full view of the world, he could do no less than magnanimously stop in order to try persuasion.

Screeching rubber tracks on the concrete and tanks skidding to a stop just a few yards in front of the sitters would climax the first test of their courage to "negate" all threats of violence. Affinity groups would have expected more scare tactics after the jet, but certainly anyone sitting close enough to the front to see the tanks would have been frightened. Among the relatives and other supporters standing in back of the aprons there would have been some screaming and fainting. But as soon as sitters caught their breath and began to smile, monitors would remind them that, as planned, now was the moment to applaud the army for its good sense in stopping. Thousands of resisters would stand up, clap their hands over their heads and cheer.

At first all hatches would stay closed as a precaution against a surprise attack, helicopters re-scrutinizing the woods for signs of an ambush or snipers. Then, after an "all clear" report, the commanding general might stand up in his hatch, getting more applause and greetings shouted in his own language: "Good morning!" "Thanks for stopping!" Reporters from the sidelines would rush to him with questions such as: Was it he who gave the order? Would he try to clear the highway? Or go through the woods?

The commanding general might refer all questions to his superior in command of the overall operation of the "West Atlantic Peace Army of Axis X." That general, in his headquarters in a Newport News motel, conferring in code with his tank commander, might order the public relations officer of the motorized division to persuade the resisters to leave. They would give the personable, English-speaking captain a genial welcome, not only because he represented discussion rather than violence, but also as a good opportunity to educate the invaders.

In fact, they would begin at once to use this whole respite as such an opportunity. They would try to fraternize with the tank crews who were climbing outside their cramped vehicles to relax. Women and men resisters with chocolates and flowers would walk across the blue line amongst the crews, offering gifts and repeating the memorized "Good morning." The tank general would have no objections — as yet! — to this fraternization, seeing it as part of the friendliness already begun by his PR (public relations) captain. But lest the army be concerned about security, resisters would be in small groups, not over four, easily watched for hidden weapons. The distribution of leaflets would be very open, no attempts being made to hide them in with flowers and candy against ANAVET's policy of no deception.

However, this could pose a dilemma if the soldiers did not want to be seen accepting literature. They might be willing to see it, even eager, yet be forbidden to read "enemy lies." Individual resisters could cope in various ways. Some might read aloud the Axis X language leaflet as best they could. Or read one stuck to a nearby turret. Better yet, they might summon one of their resister/interpreters scurrying from group to group, to conduct a real, if brief, conversation. One topic might be the leaflet already dropped, offering sanctuary to defectors. The woods on each side of the strung-out columns might be suggested as possibilities.

Only about a third of each affinity group near the front would mingle with soldiers while the rest would listen to the plea of the PR captain to let the tanks continue. Like his superiors, he would sincerely believe Fort Knox made tritium triggers for nuclear missiles secretly scattered throughout the U.S. He might present "plausible" reasons that this could be possible: Some former Pentagon admirals and generals, opposed to total disarmament, ran a secret operation known to only a few in Washington! He would plead that tanks be allowed to assist Axis X paratroopers already at Knox to open it for inspection.

After he finished there might be scattered, polite applause for the seemingly honest presentation of a sensational fantasy only some duped citizen of Axis X could believe. In the question period, asked why satellites showed no possible movements of materials at Knox, he might reply that Axis X's own satellites *did* show this. After discussing his plea all affinity groups would decide to stay. He might be impressed by their determination and courage, and later dismayed when his general refused to say no resisters would be crushed by a tank.

But the tank general would first try some "humane" means of dislodging the sitters. His first choice might be water cannons. In New York the only use of water jets had been by troopships against the smaller boats of the symbolic blockade. On Manhattan streets tanker trucks would have been blockaded by cars but here on the open highway, where army tanks could crush such obstacles, water tankers could be useful. Equipped with nozzles mounted on their tops and high-pressure pumps, they themselves might have tracks instead of wheels. Let us suppose three of them move to the front to face the sitters, one on the grassy center divider and two on the outer concrete lanes.

As soon as the nozzled vehicles are sighted the affinity groups would re-form to resist water jets. Monitors would remember from practice sessions that the ideal front-rows repulser was a robust, wiry male of average height. Seniors, women, and others least like this ideal would be assigned to the third row and beyond where they would have the important function of pressing against the first two rows to hold them in place. All rows within estimated jet range would lie on their sides with backs to nozzles. Instructions from the van would be something like:

> Monitors will see that each of you is like a shingle on a roof, overlapping and being overlapped, your feet towards the center of the highway, your back to the water. You shield the man nearest your head, below his rib cage, holding on to his coat or jacket with your higher hand. You lie so that your lower arm is free on your exposed side, to be used as needed to hang on, or shield your head. Your lower backside is similarly shielded by the man nearest your feet. Before the water hits, you press your head tight against the man you're shielding, just to one side of his hard spine. (See figures E and F.)

In this "shingled roof" formation of resisters lying apron-to-apron, monitors would choose one central apex from which bodies would lie in opposite directions, as from the ridge of the roof. This apex would be of two sitters, also with backs to nozzles but having in their laps the two hips of the adjacent prone men, thus shielding the latter's groins with the sitters' bent backs.

All loose items, chairs, cameras, purses, glasses, signs, and shoes, would be passed to the sides and rear for holding. Even pillows when soaked could be flying hazards. Probably blankets would be allowed only to those on the center divider, to be used as shields against its stones and rocks. Because such injuries presumably would not be intentional, this would not be deemed a violation of ANAVET's policy against protective gear.

The three nozzles might make practice swings, aiming high and raining chilly water on several rows. There would be the usual cries of people caught in summer showers. Then the nozzles would lower to hit

Figure E. Water jet resisters (close-up). *Sanchez*

hard at the front row. The apex men, sitting in the middle of the divider, would bend their backs as low as possible. Front row men who were farthest from a nozzle and deflecting only a glancing jet would be pounded least. Those hit more squarely would be pushed back towards the second row. If the row held, three nozzles might concentrate on one or two men to dislodge them. But front resisters would probably be more vulnerable to glancing jets coming towards the apex, as when wind drives rain up under shingles. Such jets, getting between the resister's face and the back it was pressing, might break some holds.

Reporters and photographers on the sidelines and in helicopters above, well to the sides lest they be shot down, would be broadcasting worldwide. Higher above would be a UN team and, above them, spy satellites. Perhaps hundreds of millions of TV viewers might see a front row resister who had been torn loose assume a fetal position, see him "jet propelled" over several rows behind. Because monitors had wisely located the apex at the center, the two outer nozzles could strike only limited parts of the row in the "wrong" direction.

Cameras might find more activity on the center divider where a trench could form as jets scoured away the red soil and gravel. The two apex sitters might slide into it first, and then those prone, who would lift their heads to breathe whenever the water level got too high. If the trench got too deep it would actually protect those in it, and the jet(s)

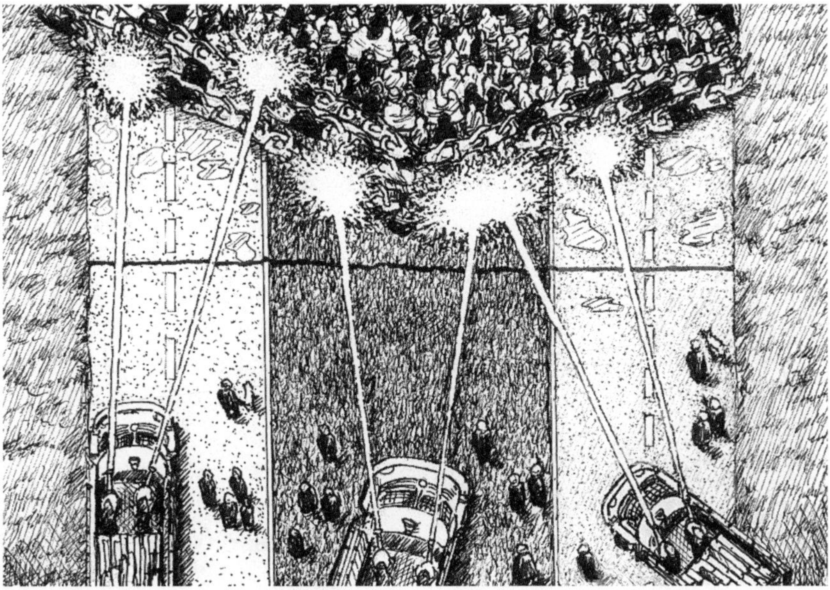

Figure F. Water jet resisters (above). *Sanchez*

might raise to hit the second row. The news media would probably pay scant attention to the sound van's message to the water tankers, its words only slightly louder than the noisy jets: "You are mistreating unarmed and defenseless civilians."

But something more than reprimands might be coming over to the army. An affinity group from a row far in the rear, bored with doing nothing, might work its way along an apron, then in the woods, cross the line to the army side. If still unnoticed by guards, they would try to walk quietly from the edge of the woods to the commanding general standing in his hatch.

"Many of us are cramped and shivering," their interpreter would say to him, "and ask you to shut off the water. You cannot hose off the highway all the way to Fort Knox, and no secret weapon is going to save us or hurt you. Because there is none."

The surprised general would order guards to escort the interlopers across the blue line. Guards would rebuff any attempts to dialog, fraternization having been ordered to end. But if an English-speaking guard happened to venture a "Go back where you belong," a resister could say "You should go back to where *you* belong." Guards would be carrying or dragging their captives, ANAVET policy being to refuse orders backed by violence, in this case by whatever arms the guards were carrying.

Meanwhile the front row might be partially or entirely re-formed or replaced by the second row, and the general would see this could continue indefinitely. Rather than be embarrassed by his tankers running dry he would save face by ordering bayoneters to replace them. His PA system would announce: "Pedestrians continuing to obstruct highway U.S. 60 will now be escorted off by infantry forces of the motorized division. No civilian moving to outside the aprons as directed will be injured in any way. Vehicles will follow in close order."

Hundreds of bayoneters would come to the front. Tank drivers would rev their diesels. Soaked resisters would leave to change clothing, and all rows would move forward to form a new front sitting thirty-five feet ahead of the line of lowered blades just starting to come forward. Resisters would try to look up seriously but not severely into the eyes of the nervous young soldiers, realizing this was probably a first time for them too. But bayoneters would avoid all eye contact and look for places to jab.

While a principle of ANAVET would be not to obey an unjust command, and so cooperate with evil, bayonet resisters would feel little compromise if, ordered to disperse, they laid back when a blade touched. In fact, the farther back a resister bent, the less able to "disperse" would that person be. This would be different from a standing position where, in giving way to blade pressure, the resister moves in the direction intended by the bayoneter. Overall the highway confrontation between bayoneters and sitters in rows would be different from the rough and tumble action depicted on decks in New York. Here, as probably first the men and then the women, felt blades pushing their shoulders, they would lean farther back. Many might hold out their arms, but only in plea fashion and not to deflect weapons. When pricked they would readily cry out whenever in pain as part of ANAVET policy of always letting adversaries know exactly what they are doing.

Also letting them know would be the van's PA, reprimanding the troops for hurting unarmed civilians defending their homeland, and any shedding of their blood, and again offering sanctuary to soldiers who defected rather than obey the unjust order. The general in turn might order more revving of motors to drown out the "enemy propaganda" — and cries of the injured — if the army PA system's patriotic music was not loud enough.

Bayoneters might next be ordered to prick legs. The injured would limp to aprons for first aid, monitors moving sitters from behind into vacancies. Reporters at aprons would film closeups of bleeding legs, and any TV interviews would be translated by the van and given back to the soldiers and tank crews. Victims, if asked if they would like to throw a rock from the apron at their bayoneter, would say no; that soldiers too were victims of a system, and should be won over, not antagonized. The general would be enraged by what got back to him of all this, and he would order all reporters and photographers to leave the area immediately, declaring that all helicopters within two thousand feet would be shot down.

He would know this might stop the world from hearing sounds but not from seeing sights via satellites. He might glance upward, then at the woods. Trees, especially if in leaf, could hide more of the operation. He would know he could switch to the woods any time, as could the enemy, and there, as his tanks flattened trees they could also flatten bodies, as in Beijing. Or his bayoneters could quietly run them through. Or shoot them, the noise drowned out by the roar of his tanks and his own helicopters overhead and the crashing of timber.

As he might toy with committing a massacre he might also be noticing how his lieutenants were rotating his front line of bayoneters, moving them back and replacing them with fresh ones. Perhaps all the noise he had ordered was drowning out the yelling of the lieutenants to jab harder? But there would be no drowning out of the problem greater than that of reporters: morale. Increasingly, soldiers would be losing their will to fight. He might do some unsettling arithmetic: Rotation of his ten thousand soldiers against replacements by many thousands of undaunted resisters. Originally he probably had not expected that his "stabbers" would have to make good their threats, and would have to cut women as well as men. And his own tank TV had a live broadcast showing the victims getting medical attention near the last rows while awaiting more ambulances to return from Richmond.

Perhaps the general might see that this PR problem for Axis X, along with his problem of morale, could be much reduced by a tear gas blitz. He would know how in Manhattan the army ran out of gas because the enemy did not scatter but stepped backwards in orderly rows. But here on the open highway, assuming supporters on aprons scattered out of the way, teams of canister throwers could race along aprons and throw between rows, forcing blockaders to run to the sides. Then his air-filtered tanks could race through before the gas cleared. Let us assume that if there were no unfavorable winds, he would order the bayoneters withdrawn and fresh infantry from carriers to come forward with canisters.

Resisters would applaud when the bayoneters withdrew, as they did when the tanks had stopped. But the jubilation would fade when they saw gas-masked soldiers with canisters race forward along both aprons. As the general had foreseen, supporters and relatives would scramble between the parked cars to clear the aprons. First the van, then the monitors, would call for volunteers from beyond the third row to run to the aprons to block. Much of the gas intended to remove the highway rows would be diverted to removing these apron blockers. Each one, holding a handkerchief and closing eyes, could stay only momentarily and would have to stumble towards the woods and join the supporters. As much as possible in the rough and tumble they would try to hold hands lest anyone trampled needed help. But as each blocker left the apron a replacement would arrive. Monitors would see that all apron space ahead of the soldiers was filled.

The regular highway rows would be on their feet moving backwards to maintain their seven-foot spacing. Front rows, hit first by gas, would try as much as possible to close eyes, hold handkerchiefs to noses, put arms on shoulders and step backwards, as in Manhattan. But here, with grenades thrown between rows, they would have to move much faster, even run, to escape the gas. Also differing from Manhattan would be the weeds of the dirt divider, where back-stepping would be more difficult than on pavement. Resisters who needed more fresh air than others in a row could leave to join a row farther back. The only masks on the defenders' side of the blue line would be those worn by the news media and by the crew of the van, itself not blocking the highway and needing at all times to be able to speak to the army. But the van probably could not adequately direct the orderly retreat of so many resisters. With even monitors "blind," training sessions with varieties of tear gases would have been highly important.

A dense gas, or east wind blowing it so there was no space into which resisters could retreat, could break up even a fast orderly retreat, causing rows to loosen arms and run to aprons to join others escaping into the woods. There, in the fresh air, monitors could lead their affinity groups to the last row, where most victims join new arrivals from Richmond, where a few go to recover. This assumes that the horn-blowing, revved-up tanks were closely following the throwers, filling in all space left by retreating resisters. But if there were ample room between, groups from the woods might move into the gas-free space to form a new front row ahead of the old one. Throwers might then be ordered to retreat to throw more gas behind themselves.

After five minutes, when his tank had advanced only twice that far in yards, the general might see there would be no breakup to rush through. The blind, coughing blockers were being replaced so fast that his throwers could not race ahead as expected. The effect of one canister could last about twenty minutes. Gas, used sparingly, would merely make resisters move backwards; used generously, they could re-form at the rear. The enemy, he would have discovered, disliked gas as it had water and bayonets but, as with them, was not afraid of it. He would realize that even if his breakthrough had succeeded, there would be more such groups on the 675 miles to Fort Knox. They could drain all the army's water and all its gas. And, if a decision were made to bayonet them, too much of the army's morale.

What the general would do next would depend greatly on that individual's personality. One commander-in-chief might decide to atom bomb the city of Hiroshima, another might not. In this worst-case scenario our general would now decide to use his tanks. He would order the gas throwers removed and the noise of horns and revving stopped so his announcement could be clearly heard:

"The Motorized Division has interrupted its scheduled trip to Fort Knox in order to make several humane attempts to clear away pedestrians illegally interfering with traffic on Highway 60. To those who have already left, we extend our thanks. Those still remaining do so entirely at their own risk. Vehicles of the Division will resume their travel in ten minutes; which gives ample time for pedestrians to move themselves and their belongings off the highway. The commanding officer of the Division will assume no responsibility for anyone who chooses to remain."

Resisters might be chuckling about references to traffic laws and to pedestrians who had left. Those absent would be the dozens with bayonet wounds, severe gassing, and some who, nearing the end of their shift, felt the need to return to Richmond for rest. Some of the "jet set," the name given resisters pummeled by water, might also have felt the need of a warm bed. Monitors would use the ten-minute period to move all resisters who had been in any of the actions to rear rows, and to unite or re-form original affinity groups as necessary. All rows would move towards the front, and entirely different sitters would now be facing the tanks from new front rows. As they saw hatches closing they would get reminder instructions from their group monitors:

"Try to look steadily and directly into the periscope of the tank coming at you, into the eyes of the driver, a fellow human being with us in a common crisis. A fellow human who does not want to hurt unarmed people. We try to look serious and unafraid, not expecting to be hurt, but all groups here have agreed that anyone who sees the tracks getting too close and wants to leave, is entirely free to do so.

"Just before the periscopes are too close for drivers to see you, monitors will signal when to lie back flat."

This lying flat would indicate to the driver getting a last view of a front row that resisters were not intending to scamper out of the tank's way. For resisters between a tank's tracks it would avoid unnecessary head injuries. Resisters lying flat would spread legs to touch feet with neighbors, extend arms to touch hands.

10

Scenario: Tanks Advance and Resisters Employ Nonviolent Action

So far we have presumed that the preceding actions were occurring during daylight. Let us say night has now fallen and the army has the advantage of being less easily photographed. Tank headlights might be beaming brightly, then switched off when an injury was actually occurring. News photographers who had sneaked back into the woods would expect any spotlights of their own to be shot out.

After the allotted ten minutes the lead tanks of the three columns, horns blaring again, would inch forward in creeper gear. Each of their three drivers would stare apprehensively into their periscopes, watching the front row of resisters lean back as the picture neared the bottom of the scope's view. We can imagine that the general's driver calls out to him that "the people aren't moving!" and is told to maintain speed. The same command would go to the other two drivers calling in the same report. Soon all would see the next rows also going prone. Probably none of the drivers or other crew members or the general would really believe that any civilian would deliberately stay to be crushed, in spite of the obstinacy shown when attacked by water jets, bayonets, and gas.

Inside the heavy tanks there would be no feel of bodies being crushed, no shrieks of pain above the blaring horns. But soon all within the three tanks would be aware of a heavy pounding on their armor.

"Ha!" the general might exclaim hopefully. "They're signaling to negotiate." As he ordered the tanks to stop he would get a report from the one behind that people were climbing up on his deck and hitting his hatch with rocks and bottles.

Pressing his hatch release, he would cautiously stand up as the lid opened and pounding ceased. In the glare of floodlights hand-held by courageous photographers, he would see enraged resisters around him pointing down at the carnage and screaming "Back up!" "Release victims!" "Back up!"

When the determined resisters had lain back before the one-mile-an-hour oncoming tanks, probably most would have thought death a remote possibility. From studies of similar confrontations the more optimistic might have expected all tanks to stop and later turn around as the Soviets had done at the Upa River. This was not Beijing, where demonstrators turned violent, and where the world could not see what was happening. True, railroad blockaders like Brian Willson and others had come close to death, but tanks can stop much more quickly than trains. The less optimistic could remember Bapu Gano in 1930 who, even while strictly maintaining his satyagraha, was deliberately crushed to death by a truck. The general in command of the tanks here could be the exception to the statement that no general today would, in full view, violate a UN article against "making war on civilians."

Resisters with their limbs extended could lie flat between the tracks, and on a flat surface not be hurt. Even an extended arm which was between the adjacent cleats of a track might be untouched. But any part of a body lying directly under a cleat would presumably be crushed beyond repair. Let us assume in this worst-case scenario that all three lead tanks run over the first row, killing several before stopping.

We need not assume that the general looking down at the carnage never saw it happening. He might have seen the bloody crushing on his tank's TV screen via his own observation helicopters, or from news photographers broadcasting live to the whole world — the same ones now alternating their lights and cameras between him and the victims, openly ignoring his threat.

"Back up! Back up!" he would hear people all around his tank and on top of it, yelling.

"People are caught underneath!" others would be shouting and pointing.

Waving away the lights in his face and venturing close to the edge of the deck, he might first see a woman lying near the front of a track, her extended leg caught under it and her face grimacing up at him. A civilian medic would already be kneeling to administer a pain killer. Looking down towards the rear he would see a front row man similarly caught, but crushed closer to his shoulder and hip. But when he glanced at the track of the neighboring tank he would see no pain, only a lifeless arm and leg extending from a totally flattened body, and perhaps some blood. There might be two such fatalities under the track on the other side of his own tank, which the shouting resisters would make room for him to see.

"All right, I'll reverse if you promise to clear my highway!" he would shout back.

His lieutenant aide at the controls, in command of the tank when the general was not aboard, would immediately order all horns stopped and the translator to stand in the hatch and render the general's offer in English on the tank's PA. But the aide could see that the highway ahead was all commotion. There were no more rows, and people were rushing about. Medics were getting out of vans pulling up in front of the tanks, obviously intending to stay until the victims were released. With the general trying to negotiate amidst the screams of victims, we can imagine the aide himself taking the initiative to break the deadlock by giving an order to back up, as slowly as possible so the general could countermand.

But the superior might make no objection, merely grabbing a turret gun to steady himself. Then, aware that resisters had stopped yelling at him, he would realize the tank was backing up.

"All right, I'm reversing, because you have promised to clear it!"

As the tank reversed it would uncover not only more gore but more shrieks of pain, and there would be more screams of horrified onlookers, more shouted orders of medics and helpers. The general, looking down at the emerging carnage, might be dazed, experiencing a psychic numbness protecting his consciousness from pain and his body from vomiting. Probably never in his career would he have seen such wanton cruelty. In some wars he might have seen hundreds or thousands of blasted civilian corpses, but here was no smoking debris to dilute the excruciating gore. Here, only blood itself covered the flattened remains of flesh and bone, of unarmed men and women who had willingly put their lives in his hands. But he might still be able to hide his shock with more shouting.

"Stupid idiots, who could easily step out of my way! Remember, you have promised to clear it!"

The other two tanks would similarly back up. We might assume that their commanding officers, unsure about running over civilians, had lagged slightly behind in the advance and run over only the first row. But they would not have had any TV screens to show actual crushing, lest some squeamish driver put on the brakes. Yet when the lying-back sitters disappeared from the periscope picture this almost reflexive braking might have occurred. A driver who had been led to believe that the enemy would move out of the way could crack up and be unable to continue.

With the backings-up the resisters would appeal for army medical help, perhaps shouting "Red Cross" in either language and making the sign and pointing to the scene. Many would run past the first three tanks, conveying the appeal via periscope and going back as far as personnel carriers. The sight of the enemy freely running from across the boundary would make the feeling contagious that all rules were for the moment suspended. With no official orders from the general, medics with stretchers would emerge from doors and hatches and run to the victims, there to administer analgesics, apply tourniquets and, perhaps under the supervision of a doctor from either side, sever the portion of a limb flattened into the concrete so the victim could be removed.

Because affinity groups would be broken apart for the emergency — some victims, some with first-aid training, some without but able to carry stretchers — the van's PA would be crucial in supervising logistics: "Clear outside eastbound lane for arriving ambulances. Clear outside westbound lane for all departing vehicles. All parked vehicles, except vans and station wagons for loading at the front, should stay in place until called for later. All rows up to eleven should clear area for loading, except those whose help is needed. Drivers stay tuned to 1020 for police siren convoy instructions."

Out of reach of the van would be the last rows. There, the center divider, separated from the two outside traffic lanes by the inner ones, would be used for medi'copters from Richmond hospitals, its parked buses and cars removed. The hospitals, already treating bayonet victims, would be prepared for an emergency, but ANAVET policy would be *not* to have ambulances or medi'copters waiting near a blockading. The principle involved would be similar to that for not wearing protective gear: When confronting an adversary the nonviolent resister does not indicate that brutality is anticipated, that the opponent is anything less than a humane and decent human being.

Resisters' supporters — spouses and other family members, and friends — would provide much help in major emergencies. Unable for many reasons to assume the risks of being ANAVET defenders, yet watching close by from or near their parked cars, they could offer personalized transportation and comfort to victims with minor injuries. Indeed, many supporters might already have given rides to Richmond for victims of bayoneting and excessive gassing. Some pre-instructions might have been given to minimize traffic obstruction by supporters who could be over-zealous and/or emotional in their assistance.

Over-eager reporters could also make problems, but dedicated resisters would want all brutality to be as widely known as possible, even at the cost of delayed medical attention to themselves, to strengthen the world boycott of the aggressor. Let us imagine an interview with a survivor, in this case fortunately unscathed because of lying completely in between a pair of tracks:

REPORTER: Mrs. Atwater, what were you thinking when you heard the screams of people on each side of you being mangled?

ATWATER: I'd been repeating the twenty-third Psalm to myself even before the tank moved over us, and I was saying it louder when we were lying there and didn't know if the headlights were off or we were under. . .

REPORTER: Yes, they were switched off.

ATWATER: And the horns got louder and I must have been yelling "The Lord is our shepherd" as loud as I could and knowing God was with us even under that tank, and it was making noise, too — all that machinery and motor — but on top of us — I don't remember how deafening. I guess I wasn't listening.

REPORTER: Has your faith in ANAVET national defense been shaken by all this? The radio says there are eight dead so far and over a dozen seriously wounded.

ATWATER: Oh no. When we all believed in shooting wars we wouldn't stop believing in it every time eight soldiers got killed. And if we'd been having a shooting war here against the tanks with our tanks and artillery and bombers to hold them back for five hours we might have lost lots more than just eight soldiers. Perhaps hundreds!

REPORTER: In a five-hour battle, easily. But a fighting soldier has an equal chance. This slaughter seems so unfair, so foolish, as if you wanted to die. How do you answer the London writer who said nonviolent resisters have martyr complexes? Maybe quite unconsciously.

ATWATER: History's conditioned the world to think soldiers aren't foolish because they want to kill other soldiers. So if the war here was equal, both sides would lose a hundred, and is two hundred dead less foolish than only eight?

REPORTER: Do you think the tanks will crush more of you?

ATWATER. If you're asking will we still be here . . . King said blood may have to flow on the streets before we're free, but it must be our blood.

REPORTER: Thank you, and you too, Mrs. Atwater, for delaying your trip back to Richmond. Have a good rest.

Worldwide TV coverage of the shocking, viewer-discretion-is-advised scenes would serve to bring in the last nations holding out against total economic isolation of Axis X. The UN trade embargo resolution would not ask for a military enforced blockade, but simply that no nation buy from or sell to Axis X anything other than food and medicine. But no such sickening pictures would be seen inside X itself. Initially it would claim, as did China immediately after Tiananmen Square, that no such incident ever happened, that no lives were lost. Later it might claim the photos were faked, made in Hollywood which had made violent horror TV films for decades. Finally, when Axis X could no longer keep out the news, it might issue its own version: "While the motorized division was traveling on the open highway with lights out as protection against secret missiles, several intoxicated pedestrians, ignoring many horns, wandered onto the highway. All vehicles immediately stopped to give medical help to the injured."

After the dead and injured had been removed from the front there would be anxious and emotional speculation by all remaining civilians about the double question: Will the tanks advance again, and if so, how soon?

But monitors of affinity groups in front rows would not be waiting for answers. Even as reporters were asking resisters if they thought Axis X would turn the tanks around because of world indignation, monitors would ask for volunteers to sit in line with tank tracks. Here there would obviously be degrees of hurt. Some might be willing to lose a left arm and leg, and monitors could place adjacent resisters so that only their extended arms and legs were crushed. But there might be volunteers who wanted to sit squarely in front, believing that deaths were needed to stop the tanks because the army might even continue if it thought it was only maiming people. The re-formed groups would have sympathy and understanding for any who felt they had to leave — probably most of them had already left before the massacre. Some of those, inspired by the courage they witnessed, might now ask to rejoin.

Around the world others could be similarly inspired. The van might announce more groups trained in nonviolent action were planning to come to Highway 60: a Bertrand Russell Peace Brigade from Britain, a Gandhi Brigade from South Africa, a Tolstoy Brigade from Russia, etc. Other news from the van's PA would include confirmation that the army helicopter in the dark had taken the general back to headquarters in Newport News, and that some soldiers had walked into the woods as deserters without being fired on!

What the tanks would do next could be as much a question inside of them as outside. Their commanding officers would learn that a colonel was now in charge instead of the general, but no new orders had been issued except to open hatches and stop idling motors. Crews would emerge to relax cramped bodies and battleground emotions. Exchanging gossip, they would hear that the general had seemed more dazed than angry, heedlessly gesturing with his revolver in a hazardous fashion, etc.

After all injured had been taken away, the gruesome job of removing the eight bodies would be left to the Richmond undertakers. Adhering to their professional standards, they would insist their operations be screened from view and that no one try to take pictures. Carefully they would pick up all of the remains except blood, which they expected the highway department to scrub away. But before all evidence of the atrocity was removed, monitors would be circulating among affinity groups to relay ideas for a unique funeral service: a memorial observance on the exact site of the horrendous deaths.

Some resisters would argue that the army should see and be reminded of the carnage. Others might feel that the dead should be honored, not exploited, that a televised spectacle on a highway would cheapen life. Advocates might counter that many military dead were in public view — tombs of unknown soldiers, and Arlington National Cemetery, that ANAVET heroes, no less than military ones, deserved to have their sacrifices widely known, not quietly forgotten. But all would agree that there should be no political oratory, and of course that the final decision would be up to the next-of-kin.

Families had no objections, some saying they would have their own church's services in addition. But they asked the same question that had underlain previous discussions: Would the tanks wait that long? Allowing an enemy to collect its dead might be an old military custom, but a cease-fire for a funeral on the battle field? Resisters had already agreed they would not ask for any delay; the request that the tanks turn around and go home would still stand. Then a suggestion might arise: *Before* the tanks turned around, their crews could be invited to attend a joint bilingual memorial which would include their fallen sniper victims. Let us assume all affinity groups would be enthusiastic, and that an invitation would be extended to army headquarters to attend the next-day services. The staff in Newport News would not reply, but would send the invitation on to Axis X leaders. There, the plan to have such a funeral would be publicly denounced as a ploy to delay the tanks in their "world peace mission." The Secretary of ANAVET Defense might smile and make no rebuttal.

Lacking any indications of army intentions, resisters would assume the tanks would wait. Morticians, lining up their caskets at the front, would assume the same, without seeming to fear being hosed, gassed, bayoneted, or run over. Richmond florists, themselves non-resisters, when arranging their displays would assume no harm would be theirs. Across the line the tank crews, seeing the chairs being set up, would also assume the army was not advancing. The colonel in charge, possibly feeling there was some agreement he was not privy to, would find it convenient to make the same assumption.

The new commander already would have had the three front tank crews returned to Newport News and their tanks sent to the rear for scrubbing off the flesh and blood. Other crews would be discussing the massacre, their revulsions, and a sense of betrayal that instead of saving the world from some secret weapon they were reduced to grinding up unarmed men and women in cold blood. They would also wonder how the deserters were faring. On the next day some might have liked to attend the memorial service, but were prohibited from sitting in the chairs set up for the army. But from behind them they could watch each white dove released when a name was read in two languages, and hear the van's translation of prayers of thankfulness for the courage of the fallen, a prayer of forgiveness for "the civilians and soldiers whose false sense of duty told them to kill." The word "snipers" was not used.

Back home the leaders of Axis X would hear no such quiet and loving reproach, only the screaming outrage of an incensed world. Their War Room brass would be discussing Geneva Convention 3.1: that noncombatants "in all circumstances be treated humanely." In a war crimes trial would non-retaliating resisters be considered non-combatants, or would resisting be combating? They would discuss Nuremberg Law: Those carrying out orders from superiors to commit atrocities are themselves guilty. The brass would be wondering if tank officers and crews might refuse orders to crush more bodies; if there would be more desertions. They would know of the clandestine interview given by a name-withheld crew member to a reporter at the edge of the woods: "I'm glad I was a gunner, not a driver!"

When the funeral ended with no trace of hate oratory leading to angry rock-throwing at tanks, the brass would not have even a flimsy excuse for killing more blockaders. But in our scenario let us assume that in the Axis X War Room there is a creative military solution to the dilemma of what to do next. Not a logical solution, such as negotiating an end to the dispute would be.

Because of the international boycott of all its international flights, Axis X would have a surplus of long-range planes. These could carry tank guns and mountings and parachute them at Fort Knox. Tanks could be turned around and dismantled inside Patrick Henry International Airport in occupied Newport News. The plan would save face; the army could announce it was switching to aircraft to avoid delays resulting from illegal use of Virginia highways by pedestrians. The plan was implemented immediately.

At the front there would be cheering and applauding the army for turning around, and some crews might wave back from their hatches. Both sides would sense great relief after many anxious hours of wondering if and when the tanks would advance again. But the resister's jubilation would be tempered by knowing that they had merely delayed the invader, that the defense would shift from an open highway to an airport and to Knox itself. Many from rear rows who had seen no action would plan to board buses to join international volunteers already gathering outside the occupied Fort's chain link fence. The highway delay would have given the latter group valuable time to organize their camping facilities and make plans. Already they might have tried to negotiate some kind of joint international inspection of the vault, and been refused by the gold-hungry leaders of Axis X. Machine gun fire between the besieged vault guards and the paratroopers would be continuing.

Most of the other fifteen thousand highway resisters would be conferring with the visiting Secretary of ANAVET Defense to plan retaking Patrick Henry airport. Many residents of nearby Williamsburg and occupied Newport News, who had done nothing to stop the tanks but were now inspired by the heroism of U.S. 60 resisters, might wish to join in. Some could now be feeling that Newport News caved in too easily to threats of shelling. "So what if they bombarded our Colonial Williamsburg!" one of its residents might remark. "We restored it once before from ruins. We could do it again!" Newport News high schoolers might already be carrying signs outside the army's motel headquarters, and getting arrested by city police for blocking civilian trucks delivering officers' food.

In its occupation of the city the army would have marked a boundary line running from the airport to the James River with a razor-wire fence. The resistance might decide first to get rid of the gate where this fence crossed Highway 60 (Warwick Boulevard) in the outskirts of Newport News. The strategy would be eventually to stop Axis planes from using the airport by liberating more of the area around it. There would be a big wave of enthusiasm for ANAVET's new slogan, "Action not reaction!" — taking the offensive. Heretofore ANAVET had mostly reacted to the initiatives of the invader. A march along U.S. 60 to occupied Newport News would turn that around! Resisters would become "interventionists."

We can picture the army's gate as an open wooden frame with stapled razor wire and bare high tension cable on insulators. As the world watched the marchers with their posters it would see them stop one hundred yards from the gate, behind which would be perhaps two hundred soldiers, In back of those guards and behind a line drawn by city police would be many hundreds of Newport News supporters of the intervention. Their banner, "Newporters for Ending Our Berlin Wall," might have been ignored by the emboldened police over army objections.

A marcher spokesperson with translator would step to the gate and carefully poke a note on the end of a plastic rod through the wires. The sound van accompanying the march would reveal the note's contents in both languages:

> Good afternoon. We greet you people wearing army uniforms as our personal friends. Our goal is the orderly end of army occupation of this city and its airport. Today we ask the removal of this gate and fence. Your army has ignored requests by many Newport News citizens that this gate stay permanently open and its guards be removed. We will wait here for the army's answer.

This note is signed by 'Nonviolent Interventionists Marching on U.S. 60.'

A similar leaflet having already been dropped in the area, the request was well known. Ordinarily an occupation force would ignore such a demand but we may assume here that because of world indignation against the army, it might make some show of respect. A lieutenant would accept the note, and in a few minutes the army's public relations officer — perhaps the same one who had addressed the sitters a few days earlier — would read the prepared reply from staff headquarters: "Any unfortunate attempt to interfere with the boundary fence securing the contractual jurisdiction of the Fifth Motorized Division of the West Atlantic Peace Army of Axis X will be considered an attack on its private property, which property will be defended by any and all means deemed necessary. The Warwick gate is closed to all vehicular and pedestrian traffic until further notice."

The reply would be signed by the commanding general. Affinity groups would confer and, agreeing that the general was refusing further discussion, the spokesperson would announce that the gate would be "dismantled." An interventionist who was a power line worker would bring her plastic ladder, rubber gloves and pliers, and attempt to untwist the high tension flex cable near the hinges. The spokesperson would explain to the army that it was ANAVET policy not to destroy property, which a cutting of the cable might be considered.

The colonel in command of protecting the fence and gate would know that the persistent enemy could easily outlast the small supply of tear gas the army still had, and might decide to try a "humane" weapon the army had not yet used either in New York or Virginia — rubber bullets. A lieutenant would quietly instruct the kneeling guards to fire no higher than the legs of the cable "saboteur" on the other side of the gate. Photographers with the march would come in for closer views. The guards, well aware of them and big posters in their rifles' line of sight saying not to hurt more unarmed civilians, etc. might aim only at the gate's wooden frame. Marchers in the line of fire, liable to be hit by stray bullets passing through the gates' open spaces, would feel free to move as long as they felt that the army's violence was directed only at the cable dismantler and not themselves. Those who felt themselves involved in the dismantling, not merely incidental to it, might choose to stay to "negate" the violence. However, these might also feel that any bullets hitting them would be strays, not intentional, and so use blankets, etc. for shields.

If, thanks to the firing guards, the rubber discs hit only the boards of the gate, the live-wire worker might be so unnerved by the racket and hazards of being hit that she would lose the steady hand needed for untwisting. Climbing down her ladder, she would say that snipping would be safer and faster. As guards rested their rifles, her suggestion would go back to affinity groups for a decision. For "establishing trust" meant keeping promises, and one of them was not to damage the invader's property. As one monitor explained the question, "If we lie about cutting their wires, they can say we lie about secret weapons."

Some reporters would be astonished at this concern for such trivial honesty, but the delay would be short. Marchers could quickly agree that ANAVET did not rule out violence to physical property but rather the secrecy and deception usually required when otherwise nonviolent protesters destroyed property. In the present case all that would be necessary to establish trust was to give advance notice of the change in policy.

Another note would be passed through the gate:

> This is notice that, because of lethal electrical danger when high tension cables are untwisted under harassment of rubber bullets, the previously announced policy of not damaging army property will be suspended during this operation. Cable joints will be cut, but this will waste only a few inches of cable.

Loud army music might drown out the translation, but the TV world would hear it. The line worker with long, insulated cutters might be hit in the legs, or still be shielded enough by the gate frame and post, while quickly finishing her task. Others would step to the gate to remove the dead razor wire. Standing more in the open framework, many hit in the legs would have to leave. Some might need help as they hobbled back to the marchers, or even might have to be carried. Their places would be taken by new volunteers willing to be bruised.

So far in this book we have portrayed all ANAVET-trained civilian defenders of the U.S. as behaving ideally, as never being provoked into retaliating. But just as the militarist knows a gun may jam, a tank or plane malfunction, a submarine have an accident, so some people may "lose their cool." While this could happen with anyone, let us suppose that at the gate a young male is the offender. Angered by the sight of so much bruising and bleeding, he would run to the gate to scream epithets at the army. Monitors would lead him away. Unfortunately his breakdown would be featured in the TV coverage. Fortunately, if interviewed, he could explain that he would have to apologize to the soldiers before rejoining his group.

A problem in the van would be whether or not to translate "dirty rotten sons of bitches" back to the soldiers. Since some already would have understood the English, and the army PA might translate it into something even worse, the van would do so:

> To every soldier we apologize. The denunciation applies well to your cruel brutality. But you yourselves are not 'dirty, rotten sons

> of bitches.' You are persons, as we all are. And you are victims, as we all are. The way out of this tragic situation is for all of us to refuse to be violent either in words or in actions.
>
> We offer safe asylum to any of you who defect from an army ordering you to injure unarmed civilians who have a right to travel on this street.

Probably neither the cursing nor the translation would be heard above the firing and army music. But Axis X soldiers might be listening elsewhere — on hidden sets at the airport, at Fort Knox, in Newport News hotels, and even in New York. But while the van's PA was finishing, the gate's wires below four and a half feet would have been removed sufficiently to step through. Dismantling would stop, as would the shooting.

A new note would then be handed through, reminding the army that according to surrender terms it was the responsibility only of the Newport News Police Department to handle "interlopers." The entire march would move forward slowly, stopping at the gate. The officer in charge, having no orders to shoot people not harming the gate or fence, might already be planning to call the chief of police, greatly relieved to stop shooting civilians — and in turn to stop being shot by photographers while doing so.

The police chief, when contacted, could well reply that his jail was already filled with Newporters violating the occupation contract, that he was putting the overflow into a school gym. Army headquarters would be brought into the conversation:

GENERAL: How many violators are there?

GATE OFFICER: If all step across, about five thousand.

GENERAL: How many can the police lock up?

CHIEF: There's a vacant auto paint shop where I could keep maybe a hundred. But I'd need some blankets — can you spare any? All I can do with the rest is book and release on recognizance pending hearings.

After the conversation the general and staff would decide to abandon most of occupied Newport News and move into the airport, now the center of army action. Shuttling planes from Axis X could bring in all needed supplies, and city cooperation would no longer be needed. There would be no official termination of the occupation contract, but it would be dead, and the thousands of interventionists and hundreds of arrested dissidents could act freely anywhere in the city outside the airport. The airport would be ringed with tanks, their machine guns intact even though their 80 mm guns were being removed for shipment to Fort Knox. Their crews and the division's infantry would receive more rifles and ammunition, making the airport almost a fortress.

11

Scenario: Fort Knox Blasted Open and Counterinvaded

At Fort Knox, the machine gun battle between paratroopers and besieged guards would finally end after shelling of the Depository by the air-lifted 80 mm tank guns. A guard would poke a white flag up through the rubble, then crawl out between the jagged concrete blocks and twisted steel when guns fell silent. A lieutenant would advance to confer, after which all shifts of the guards would climb out, dressed in their Department of the Treasury uniforms. In excellent health, they would need only to catch up on sleep lost during the shelling which, fortunately, had been brief. Although they were technically civilians, they had surrendered in military fashion and would be treated as prisoners of war.

The capitulation would be watched by resisters outside Fort Knox's chain link fence, peering through with binoculars. All the international volunteers would now be there, raising the camp's population to over twenty thousand. They would be waiting for the vault's shooting defense to end so a nonviolent defense could begin. But let us suppose the overseas groups first join together in a last-ditch try at negotiating. A spokesperson for the Internationals with a white flag would climb over the fence the moment the shooting stopped and speak in English to the lieutenant's interpreter. He would explain that Axis X had refused the offer of the U.S. to allow two members of the UN Disarmament

Verification Commission to inspect the vault, that now the Internationals were proposing that two of their own group, not a part of the UN, and a general appointed by Axis X be allowed by the U.S. to enter.

In Washington, the proposal would meet with Treasury Department approval, but be rejected by the government of Axis X. This second rejection would confirm most world opinion that the real purpose of Axis X was not to inspect the vault but rather to steal its gold. But the Internationals would make no accusations when their suggestion was refused. They would merely announce that at the first indication of anything being removed from the vault they and the others outside the fence would enter the Depository area to prevent it.

Army bulldozers would remove some blasted concrete, and acetylene cutting equipment would be put to work making a hole in the vault itself. Ample supplies of this gas and oxygen might already have been taken from Newport News shipbuilders before that city's liberation. If not, more would have to be imported from Axis X. In our scenario with its mostly-unbelievable plot let us suppose that two high officers climb through and find nothing on either level but stacks of gold bars. Genuinely surprised, they would open their sealed instructions and learn the bullion was to be packed in special lead-sheathed boxes and flown to Axis X. All army personnel except the packers were to consider the contents to be what was stated by the warning labels, which were big enough to be read easily from the sky: "Danger — Radioactive Tritium."

High ranked army officers might be angry about being duped into the category of bank robbers — after their tanks had killed unarmed civilians — and be tempted to defect. But let us assume they are mollified by the explanation that the gold "is only fair compensation for army expense necessitated by the intransigence of the U.S. in refusing to open the vault." As soon as satellites would report boxes being loaded into army trucks at the vault, the thousands of campers outside the chain link fence would lift its posts out of dug-away holes and lay it flat on the ground. Then, on a quarter-mile front they would walk over it towards the vault, facing threatening machine guns.

Simultaneously, blocking would begin of the airstrip where the boxes would be transferred from trucks to Axis planes. Acres of junked cars, some with their wheels removed to prevent rolling, would be waiting at airports in Kentucky and neighboring states. From there they would be carried by drone cargo planes or slung under drone helicopters for dropping on Knox's runway. Computer control would prevent injury to army personnel on the ground, but broadcasts to the army would warn that malfunctioning was possible should there be anti-aircraft fire.

In Newport News resisters would take corresponding measures to block Patrick Henry International, the fueling depot for Axis planes taking the gold home. By now such shuttling planes would also be the army's only source of food, fuel for its cookstoves, etc., as in Manhattan. All airport electricity and gas would have been turned off, and no more water supplied than enough for drinking. Aerial leafleting of soldiers inside the airport, those at Fort Knox, any still aboard ships in Newport or New York, or in camps, would say the army was now hijacking gold. Bigger drone planes and helicopters would be dropping or parachuting junk cars on the International runways as at Fort Knox, those shot down now endangering civilians as well as soldiers in both areas.

The army would reduce its own hazards by using smart missiles to destroy such planes at a distance. But its supply of these sophisticated and expensive anti-aircraft weapons would make only a tiny dent in the number of U.S. aircraft available, and eventually the army would be reduced to machine gunning at closer range. Before that time the resistance might also launch barrage balloons at low altitudes outside the airport. A helium-filled gas bag big enough to lift two thousand feet of nylon rope might be easier to replace than a drone plane, depending on the quantity of gas stocked by the Department of ANAVET Defense. Many small, strung-out balloons would be a more difficult target. Hot-air balloons using ordinary methane would be more economical. ANAVET policy would require precautions to prevent actual collisions resulting in injury or death to flight crews. Cable winch bases could be on trucks, shifting positions to impair targeting by artillery and aircraft. New positions taken at night might actually entail spotlighting the top balloon to insure that the barrage was a blockade and not an unknown snare. No ANAVET policy would be violated by using trees to hide winch machinery.

At Fort Knox, the wide front of interventionists would be slowly walking towards the vault, taking care their quick dodging of shot-down aircraft and plummeting junked cars did not alarm the army guards watching from a distance. The latter might use binoculars to read the Internationals' banners, citing the names of their countries: "India," "Russia," etc. Other banners would read "Stop Stealing Gold" and, more pertinently for the guards, "Don't Be a War Criminal." Leaflets would explain the Nuremberg ruling that subordinates ordered by superiors to commit inhumane acts are guilty if they do so, and would quote Geneva Conventions Articles about harming civilian populations. (Ironically, the incoming planes being blockaded would carry "humane" weapons to replenish diminishing stocks. Guards would know that after their tear gas, rubber bullets, etc. ran out, they would be expected to use bayonets and steel bullets.)

The most interesting leaflet information, for guards and everyone else in the army, would be uncensored "home" news, supplementing clandestine listening to U.S. broadcasts. First, they might have heard that members of the United Nations Association in Axis X had openly questioned their government's story that the United States had bribed UN members to vote against opening Knox as it had bribed UN nations to vote for the Persian Gulf War. The UNA questioners, according to underground news, would have been arrested. Then there would have been satellite pictures of students' banners, as previously mentioned; those might have challenged Axis X claims that one hundred soldiers had been killed in Newport news by army bullets, or that the tank atrocity was staged, etc.

As thousands of marchers approached army guards at the vault, the same guards would get news of another march facing guns: In the capital of Axis X tens of thousands were protesting the seizure of gold. Protesters would include college students, church groups, members of underground peace organizations, and consumers venting anger at having to wait in lines for hours because of the boycott — and being told it was for "world peace." Tear gas which Axis X might now want to use at home would all have been sent abroad. Some of this gas at Knox and the airport would now be used against encroaching interventionists,

All army personnel at both places would know via the grapevine that the packers were putting refiner-stamped gold bars into the shipping boxes. Disillusioned soldiers, like other humans when morale is low, might continue for a while, out of apathetic inertia, doing what is demanded. They would fix bayonets, don masks, and pick up canisters. At the airport they would use the gas when interventionists began digging up some of the fence; at the vault, when any came within fifty yards.

At Knox, those interventionists in a gassed section of the wide front would try to retreat in orderly ANAVET formation. The unaffected might move sideways and fill in, or in the open spaces of Fort Knox continue ahead and then turn to approach the vault from a new direction. Care would be taken not to panic guards, not to let them fear they were being surrounded. But other than such precautions, there would seem to be little value in interventionists at Knox devising brilliant phalanx movements such as those that were so important to the generals on the plains of Waterloo.

The important strategy at both Knox and the airport would be the continuation of ANAVET's goal of destroying the fighting morale of the invader. To this end, confronting armed soldiers by unarmed human defenders could be more effective over all than the obstruction of runways and city streets by cars, or of airports by balloons, or piers by freighters. Even the knowledge that the whole world was boycotting the Axis might be as important for its lowering of army morale as for the economic damage of the boycott itself. And the boycott could ultimately be well over ninety percent effective. Unlike in Haiti (1994) and in Iraq (1991), we can assume Axis X has no sympathizers willing to engage in profitable black-marketeering. Even in the Gulf War, five former Secretaries of State testified before Congress that sanctions against Iraq were working.

At this point the reader might well ask why, if the boycott against Axis X might be so effective, would any resisters need to sacrifice themselves? Even the stolen gold would be worthless if no nation would sell anything! Why should people in the U.S. not live as comfortably as possible under the occupation and simply wait for the occupying power to collapse? One answer is that sanctions take time and do involve some sacrifices by the boycotters. For example, suppose Peru had been buying all of its peanuts and wrist watches from X, presumably because this was the best quality for the best price. During the boycott, Peruvians would then have to pay more for the same quality, or get less for the same prices, and they might grumble. But they might grumble more — and urge that the favorable trade agreement with X be restored if the occupied people themselves were sacrificing as little as possible.

The willingness of those invaded to die for their freedom would tend to arouse the emotions of people everywhere. True, as mentioned previously, the United States with some $300 billion saved annually from its budget could afford to assist countries in cases like the hypothetical one with Peru, countries which would suffer by joining the boycott. But it would seem risky to rely entirely on *buying* other nations' cooperation. For one thing, they might be tempted as the months passed to increase the price, given the present policy of most countries to gain for themselves as much as they can. Secondly, the invader in a cooperating occupation might soon control all international relationships and prevent such subsidies.

The world boycott of Axis X in this scenario, while important to the defense of the United States, would thus be secondary to the dedication of trained ANAVET volunteers. They alone, if necessary, could break the will of the invader and end the occupation, as did the satyagrahis in India who received no help from an international trade embargo against Britain. Hitler once said it was not enough to conquer a people — they must *know* they are conquered. In an invaded U.S. it would be the unflagging refusal to be conquered, as in nonviolent India, as in violent and shattered Vietnam, which would eventually win. In South America, nonviolent action has been called *firmeza permanente* — "relentless persistence."

At Knox, a problem for interventionists would be presented by a complete blockade of the runway that would prevent everyone, including troops, from leaving. This might be circumvented by having U.S. helicopters waiting behind the throng of civilians facing the guards, and leaflets offering safe passage to Newport News docks where army ships were still tied. Soldiers would need only walk through an opening in the civilian front, and might even be allowed to carry their rifles. Would the remaining guards shoot at any takers? For all guards the long stand-off, the facing of twenty thousand civilians while soldiers behind rushed to load heavy boxes onto trucks, would be a heavy strain. Guards could foresee no more supply planes landing with food, butane for heating and cooking, gasoline for trucks and for army helicopters to make return trips to the airport. They would know that their supplies were limited, all now having to be parachuted as in New York, that the needed tear gas was being used at home on marchers chanting "Bring troops home."

In this worst-case scenario we have assumed that the invaders do finally reach their objective and begin loading gold. Let us now assume that one plane loaded with bullion manages to take off from the almost blockaded runway, and is able to land at barraged Henry International for refueling in order to make the trip home. There the generals in command would hear on their uncensored TV news that the "tritium" boxes held gold, and would get reports from their vault crews that the bars measured 7 × 3⅝ × 1¾ inches and weighed between twenty-seven and twenty-eight pounds. They could examine the plane's boxes and see for themselves that they had been duped. From believing they had been directing a great world peace mission requiring them to kill and injure harmless civilians, they would now find themselves to be mere bank robbers. Loss of fighting morale could spread from bayonet-jabbing privates to the top echelons.

What would the dismayed and angry brass do? Even if they were willing to continue the heist, would they want to risk their first load crashing into balloon ropes and exposing the shiny gold for all the world to see? Exposing themselves as the thieves they were? They would know their situation in the airport was increasingly perilous, with supplies having to be parachuted whenever the big liners from home were unable to touch down. Should they abandon Henry International and withdraw to the ships, a move in which there was the standing offer of Newport News to cooperate? Even if Axis X planes could have enough fuel to fly round-trip to Knox, chances of loading them with gold were fast fading. The generals would know the overall situation there was as follows:

1. The runway was increasingly being blocked by junked cars.
2. Gasoline for army trucks towing away this blocking was running out.
3. Ammunition needed to down planes dropping cars was running out.
4. Tens of thousands of civilians were continually pressing towards the vault, wearying guards in face-to-face confrontations, and more civilians were arriving hourly.
5. All tear gas was used up.
6. Guards were frequently showered with UN leaflets telling of Geneva Conventions against harming civilians, of possible war crime trials for obeying orders to do so.
7. It was common knowledge among all personnel that they were handling gold, not tritium or other nuclear materials.
8. Food and potable water were running low.
9. Groups of deserting frontline guards had been welcomed into enemy helicopters and transported to Newport ships, without attempted restraint by the army.

At this point readers might like to reach their own conclusions about what the generals would do. The writer suggests that if the enemy top brass were still willing to be branded as robbers by the world, they would first follow standard military procedure and ask Axis X leaders for reinforcements at Knox. This would be tantamount to a new invasion: For clearing out civilians, thousands of replacement paratroopers, more tear gas, water cannons, etc. would be required. For clearing the runway, they would need more parachuted tow trucks and gasoline, and for the soldiers themselves, more food, water, tents, etc. This massive air invasion, the generals would know, would be all but impossible for Axis X leaders, who now were facing domestic opposition and a deteriorating economy. Their "No" would be welcome.

So far our scenario has not mentioned what would be the normal conferring between the Newport News generals and their counterparts in New York. In earlier phases it might have focused on sharing their mutually needed helicopters, transport planes, tear gas, food from Axis ports, etc. By now they would have shared the discovery that no tritium had been detected in either the Knox or Manhattan vaults, but that their Axis leaders had ordered all gold in both places be transported home. When the New York brass would learn more details of this hijacking from Knox, they could become suspicious of their government's aims and on their own decide to send Manhattan samples to Patrick Henry for analysis.

When the results were found to be negative, the invasion's commanders might decide jointly to notify Axis leaders that the missions of both invasions had now been accomplished: all suspected vaults had been forcibly opened and no evidence of tritium or any other nuclear materials had been found, and they were awaiting orders to return home. They might even suggest a face-saving statement for their government to issue:

"Samples of the metal found in all inspected vaults have been tested in the army's field laboratory in Patrick Henry International Airport, Virginia, and were determined to be free of any nuclear materials. Its mission now accomplished, all units of the West Atlantic Peace Army will begin immediate withdrawal from occupied positions in the United States."

Axis X leaders, facing future potential demands for their resignations, might well accept this way out of their misadventure — sensing that their generals would withdraw with or without official government permission. Evacuations from Knox, Henry airport, the UN and other occupied areas of Manhattan, would be scenes of celebration, with civilians and soldiers joining in the festivities. In Newport News there would be a parade with the army's tanks, minus their stripped guns, from airport to docked ships, cheered by hundreds of thousands of area residents lining the route. On the steps of New York's City Hall generals would accept the invitation from the Mayor to address a farewell celebration, followed by today's version of a ticker tape parade down Broadway. Troops would be feted in cafes, nightclubs, and block parties.

Thus the low fighting morale of the soldiers would be replaced by a new morale — the good feelings people know when they have done a good deed. The soldiers' dejected moods, after being reprimanded by outsiders, and tormented by inner guilt for doing the wrong thing, would give way to an elation that results from people's congratulations and from the satisfaction of knowing one has done the right thing. If, as said earlier, the main purpose in an ANAVET defense is to destroy the attacker's morale, it would not be the ultimate goal. During withdrawal the respect for human personality would go beyond mere refusal to retaliate, defenders now making every effort to restore a sense of self-worth.

This cheering send-off, reminiscent of that for British soldiers sailing from India after independence, would help to offset negative troop receptions at home by disillusioned citizens who might be resentful about what their army had done. Back in Axis X many veterans perhaps would fulfill the peacetime goal of ANAVET: converting other nations to its principles. Veterans with the U.S. experience would be ideal crusaders. In their face-to-face confrontations they would have felt the contagious effect of the defenders' unfaltering dedication to high principles and superior courage. Any reader who, during the Vietnam war heard dissident veterans speak out against it may remember their sense of empowerment. As part of organizations like "Winter Soldiers," veterans toured the U.S., giving firsthand accounts about the atrocities they and others had committed, acknowledging that they abhorred a policy that resulted in the waste of human lives. Far from being dejected, these veterans exemplified the vigor and enthusiasm of crusaders for a great cause.

Beyond the goal of converting all nations to a policy of reliance on civilian nonviolent defense in place of military violent defense, there would be the hope of a more intelligent world in which international law would replace the anarchy of national sovereignty. Perhaps striving towards the first goal will help to achieve the second.

Conclusion

In the Preface I looked at the examples of India and Vietnam in which the losses in lives and property were far less for the victimized nation when it employed nonviolent rather than violent resistance. In Chapter 1 I examined the many other advantages for the U.S. in peacetime of an alternative to its present military preparedness program. Its published price tag is more than that of the next ten leading nations combined, and that its real, higher total cost is over one-fourth of the Federal income tax dollar. This ongoing, almost $300 billion annual expenditure is a major villain in our troubled economy with its inherently inflationary nature and the high-salaried "brain-drain" and enormous profits of the military-industrial complex which impair the competitiveness of domestic firms with those abroad. In addition, the arms industry employs fewer workers per billion dollars than any other.

We saw how the Pentagon is our most toxic polluter as well as the biggest consumer of oil. The U.S. homicide rate, many times higher than that of any other industrialized nation, matches its many-times-higher preparedness to kill. If we accept violence as valid between nations, by example it becomes valid between persons. We also saw that military violence against weaker nations, in actual intervention, proxy wars, or in arms sales, can result in retaliatory terrorism, and that future plans for more such violence abroad will result in its escalation at home.

In addition to these urgent social and economic reasons, there is a moral and religious reason for opposing violence — the act of preparing, and the willingness to engage in, the monstrous obscenity of modern warfare is in itself evil. In varying degrees, both in the religious and secular community, people feel this way, but, except for a relatively few pacifists, most have reluctantly accepted this evil as necessary for defense.

In the balance of this book we saw how this "necessity" is no longer necessary, illustrating through a hypothetical scenario that a viable alternative exists. Few of the scenario tactics were original, most being based on actual historical examples of unarmed civilians who have resisted superior armed might. However, we would probably never need to engage in such a scenario; merely convincing the world we were so prepared would deter any naked aggression based on greed. No nation or group would have any reason to attack or invade a U.S. which was no longer the domineering superpower but was the world's friendly and cooperating partner.

Nonviolent resistance is not a novel, untried idea but an old one whose implementation is needed today as never before. A revolution in the way we insure the national security of the U.S. should begin now.

Notes

NOTES FOR CHAPTER 1.

1. As a courtesy to other countries of North, Central, and South America, the author does not use "Americans" to designate citizens of the United States.
2. Eisenhower also points out that, even from only a *security* viewpoint, war spending has limits: "The military, . . . not productive itself, necessarily must feed on the energy, productivity, and brainpower of the country, and if it takes too much, our total strength declines."
3. Seymour Melman, *The Permanent War Economy* (New York: Simon & Shuster, 1985). See pp. 20, 44, 103–4, and 141.
4. Seymour Melman, quoted by Center for Defense Information, *The Defense Monitor* 21, no. 3 (1992).
5. National Science Board, quoted in a California SANE/FREEZE pamphlet, 1993. Complete source information not available.
6. Kevin J. Cassidy and Kevin B. Bean, "Military Dollars and Public Sense," *The Nonviolent Activist*, April-May 1992. Both authors are former chairpersons of the subcommittee on defense industries of the state of Connecticut's Legislative Task Force on Manufacturing.
7. Lenny Siegel, Gary Cohen, and Ben Goldman, "The U.S. Military's Toxic Legacy," *The Nonviolent Activist*, December 1992.
8. *Ibid.*
9. Rev. Dr. Martin Luther King, Jr., "Beyond Vietnam," speech given at Riverside Church, New York, NY, April 4, 1967, published in Dr. Martin Luther King, Jr., et al., *Dr. John C. Bennett, Dr. Henry Steele Commager, and Rabbi Abraham Heschel Speak on the War in Vietnam* (New York: Clergy and Laymen Concerned About Vietnam, 1967).

10. Yolanda King, interview by Tim Hughes, *WAVE*, June 22, 1994.
11. Fellowship of Reconciliation, "Stop the Killing; Start the Healing," *Leaflet*, 1993.
12. Jim Wallis, *The Soul of Politics* (Maryknoll, NY: Orbis Books in association with New York, NY: New Press, 1994).
13. *Ibid.*
14. Marion Wright Edelman, "The Children We Have in Trust," *Sojourner's*, April 1994.
15. American Psychological Association, Commission on Violence and Youth, "Violence and Youth," *Summary Report 1*.
16. John Swomley, "Cultural Despair" *Alternatives*, Spring 1994.
17. Wendell Berry, *Sex, Economy, Freedom, and Community* (New York: Pantheon, 1993).
18. Michael True, "To Reform America—The Nonviolent Solution," *Worcester Magazine*, February 16, 1994. The author has also written *Ordinary People: Family Life and Global Values* (Maryknoll, NY: Orbis Books, 1991).
19. *Los Angeles Times*, May 25, 1994. Complete source information not available.
20. Center for Defense Information, *The Defense Monitor*, 23, no. 5 (1994).

NOTES FOR CHAPTER 2.

1. Martin Luther King, Jr., *Stride Towards Freedom* (New York: Harper & Row, 1958).
2. Angie O'Gorman, ed., *The Universe Bends Towards Justice*, (Philadelphia: New Society Publishers, 1990).

NOTES FOR CHAPTER 3.

1. Bertrand Russell, "Justice in War-Time," reprinted in "War and Non-Resistance," *Atlantic Monthly*, August 1915.
2. Jessie Wallace Hughan, "If We Should Be Invaded," War Resisters League of New York, *Pamphlet*, 1940.

NOTES FOR CHAPTER 4.

1. Jonathan Schell, *Fate of the Earth* (New York: Knopf, 1982).

NOTES FOR CHAPTER 5.

1. *Harijan*, October 15, 1938. *Harijan* was a weekly newsletter that Gandhi published.

NOTES FOR CHAPTER 6.

(None.)

NOTES FOR CHAPTER 7.

1. Quoted courtesy United Press International. Complete source information not available.
2. Richard Gregg, *The Power of Nonviolence* (Nyack, NY: Fellowship Publications, 1944).
3. Allan A. Hunter, *Courage in Both Hands* (New York: Ballantine Books, 1962).
4. Andre Trocme, "The Law Itself Was a Lie," *Fellowship*, January 1955.
5. Magne Skodvin, *Civilian Resistance as a National Defense*, ed. Adam Roberts (Harrisburg, PA: Stackpole Books, 1968).
6. *Ibid.*
7. Diderich H. Lund, "Pacifism Under the Occupation," *Fellowship*, December 1948.
8. For more on the Allies' political situation, see Klaus Harppecht, *The East German Rising* (London: Thames & Hudson, 1955); also President Eisenhower, Letter to Chancellor Konrad Adenaur, July 23, 1953, printed in Department of State *Bulletin*, August 3, 1953.
9. David McReynolds, "Report from Prague," *WIN*, September 16, 1968.

NOTES FOR CHAPTER 8.

1. Bob Levering, "Stopping Ammo Trains, Portland-style," *Fellowship*, December 1972.
2. Corazon Aquino, news conference, Manila, February 26, 1986. Complete source information not available.
3. Photographers and reporters of the *Ming Pao News* (Hong Kong), *June Four, a Chronicle of the Chinese Democratic Uprising*, (Fayetteville, AR: University of Arkansas Press, 1989).
4. Alexander Pronozin, "Nonviolence Brought Down the Coup," Peace Media Service, September 28, 1991.

5. David Hartsough, "In the USSR: Faces of Courage and Hope," *Peacework*, December 1991.
6. Victoria Bunnell, et al., *Russia at the Barricades* (Armonk, NY: M.E. Sharpe, 1992).

NOTES FOR CHAPTERS 9–11.

(None.)

Index

Afghanistan, war in, 119
African National Congress, 16
Agent Orange, 7
ahimsa, 15
Allies, the, 85
Alternatives, 160 n. 16 (ch. 1)
American Psychological Association, 9, 160 n. 15 (ch. 1)
Amnesty International, 111
Amritsar (British massacre), xi, 36, 41, 57
ANAVET (Action Negating All Violence and Establishing Trust: the author's fictional resistance force), 24–25, 27, 29–31, 33, 35, 37–38, 42–48, 50–52, 54–59, 62–62, 65, 67, 69, 80, 87, 103, 105–107, 109–110, 114–115, 121–122, 124–125, 128, 136–137, 139–144, 149–152, 155
anthistemi, 16
Aquino, Corazon, 111, 161 n. 2 (ch. 8)
Associated Press, The, 86
Atlantic Monthly, 160 n. 1 (ch. 3)
Axis X (a fictional superpower in the author's example of nonviolent defense tactics), 23–69, 103–108, 123–124, 129, 138, 140, 141, 143, 145, 147, 148, 150–155
Azerbaijan, 115

Bangor, Washington, *93*, 110
Bapu Gano, 109, 134

BBC. *See* British Broadcasting Corporation
Bean, Kevin B., 5, 159 n. 6 (ch. 1)
Beckman, Mel, 12
Beijing, China, 42, *98*, *99*, *100*, 111–114, 134, . *See also* Tiananmen Square
Belgium, 77–78
Bennett, John C., Dr., 159 n. 9 (ch. 1)
Berry, Wendell, 10, 160 n. 17 (ch. 1)
blockade, 31, 34, 67
blockade, human, *94*
blockade, people's, *91*, *92*, *93*, 110
Bombay, 74
Bosnia, 13
boycott, international, 67, ; regional, 79
Brandenburg Gate, 84
Britain. *See* Great Britain
British Broadcasting Corporation, 79, 85
Bronx, 29
Budapest, 86
Buddhist monk, *90*
Bunnell, Victoria, 162 n. 6 (ch. 8)
Bureau of Labor Statistics, 5
Burlington Northern Railroad, 110
Bush, President George, 8, 67

Calcutta, the "Black Hole of," 71
Cassidy, Kevin J., 5, 159 n. 6 (ch. 1)
Caulkins, Ellanor, 109
Caulkins, Kenneth, 109
Center for Defense Information, 159 n. 4 (ch. 1), 160 n. 20 (ch. 1)
Chambon, Le, 80
Changsha, 112
Chicago Daily News, 74
Children's Defense Fund, 9
Chinese government, 111–114. *See also:* Beijing; Tiananmen Square
Christian, King, 79
Chronicle of a Night on the Barricades, A, 117–119
civil disobedience, 17
Civilian-Based Defense Association (Omaha), 12
civilian-based defense, 15, 19
civil rights campaign, 62
Cohen, Gary, 7, 159, nn. 7, 8 (ch. 1)
Cold War, 12
Commager, Henry Steele, Dr., 159 n. 9 (ch. 1)

Commission on Violence and Youth, 160 n. 15 (ch. 1)
Committee on Science and Technology, 5
Communist Party, Soviet, 116
Concord (CA) Naval Weapons Station, 111
Congressional Research Service, 12
consensus decision making, 36
Contras (Nicaraguan), 111
Czechoslovakia, 87–88, 110

Da Nang, *90*
Dandi, sea at, (India), 72
Defense Department. *See* U.S. Department of Defense
Defense Environment Restoration Program, 5
The Defense Monitor, 160 n. 20 (ch. 1)
Department of State Bulletin, 161 n. 8 (ch. 7)
Degoutte, General, 78
demoralization, troop. *See* troop morale
Denmark, 79
Dharsana Camp, 72–77
Dharsana Salt Works, 72
DOD. *See* U.S. Department of Defense
Dyer, General, 41

East Berlin, 84
East Germany. *See* German Democratic Republic
Edelman, Marion Wright, 9, 160 n. 14 (ch. 1)
Eisenhower, Dwight, 3, 4, 35, 159 n. 2 (ch. 1), 161 n. 8 (ch. 7)
England. *See* Great Britain

Federal Reserve Bank, 26
Federation of All-Beijing College Students Unions (Interim), 112
Fellowship, 80, 110, 161 n. 7 (ch. 7), 161 n. 1 (ch. 8)
Fellowship of Reconciliation, 8, 160 n. 11 (ch. 1)
firmeza permanente (relentless persistence), 152
Fjellbu, Dean, 82
Fort Knox, Kentucky, xiii, 26–27, 55, 66, 68, 103–104, 122, 124, 127, 131, 141, 145, 146, 147–154
France, 11, 77–78, 80
freedom campaign, India, 109
Freedom Fighters, 87

Gandhi, Mohandas K., Mahatma, x, xi, 15, 16, 24, 37, 41, 42, 43, 62, 72–77
Gary, Indiana, 26

Geneva Convention, 40, 140
German Democratic Republic (GDR), 83–85
Germany, 5, 17, 24, 25, 77–83
Goldman, Ben, 7, 159, nn. 7, 8 (ch. 1)
Golovko, Capt. Michael, 117
Gorbachev, President Mikhail S., 115
Great Britain, 11, 17, 71–77
Gregg, Richard, 161 n. 2 (ch. 7)
Grenada, 10, 13, 67
Gulf War. *See* Persian Gulf War

Haiti, 13
Halle, 84
Harijan, 77, 161 n. 1 (ch. 5)
Harppecht, Klaus, 161 n. 8 (ch. 7)
Hartsough, David, 115, 117, 162 n. 5 (ch. 8)
Heschel, Abraham, Rabbi, 159 n. 9 (ch. 1)
Hindus, 75
Hiroshima, 42
Hitler, 25
House Government Operations Committee, 4
Hughan, Jessie Wallace, 19, 20, 21, 25, 160 n. 2 (ch. 3)
Hughes, Tim, 160 n. 10 (ch. 1)
Hungarian Revolt of 1956, 85
Hungary, 81, 85–87
Hunter, Allan A., 161 n. 3 (ch. 7)
Hussein, Saddam, 25

India, x, 21, 37, 109, 157
Indian National Congress, 77
Iraq, 13, 25, 67
Irish Republican Army, 12
Irwin, Lord, 71
Israel, 12

Japan, 5, 24
Jena, GDR, 84, 110
Jesus, 11, 16, 17, 62
Jews, 80
June Four, 112

KGB, 116
King, Martin Luther, Jr., xi, 7, 16, 24, 37, 62, 159 n. 9 (ch. 1), 160 n. 1 (ch. 2)
King, Yolanda, 7, 160 n. 10 (ch. 1)
Komar, Dmitri, 119
Korea, 13
Korea, North, 85
Krichevskii, Igor, 119
Kuwait, 25

League of Nations, 25
Leningrad, 45
Levering, Bob, 161 n. 1 (ch. 8)
Libya, 10
Lithuania, 115
Litvinov, Maxim, 88
Litvinov, Pavel, 88
Los Angeles Times, 160 n. 19 (ch. 1)
Lund, Diderich, 83, 161 n. 7 (ch. 7)

Maps: Eastern Virginia, 104; Manhattan, 28, 39;
March to the Sea, 72
Marcos regime, 111
market economy, 4
Martindell, Anne, 32
McReynolds, David, 87, 161 n. 9 (ch. 7)
McSorley, Father Richard, S.J., 8
media, use of, 34, 121
Melman, Seymour, 4, 5, 159 nn. 3, 4 (ch. 1)
Mexican War, 25
Mexico, 25
Middle East, 9
military-industrial complex, 4, 5, 157
military, Soviet, 85
military spending, 5, . *See also* U.S. military budget
Miller, Webb, 72
Milorg, 81, 83
Ming Pao News, 161 n. 3 (ch. 8)
Moscow, *101*, 115; August coup, 116, 121
murder statistics, 8

Nagy, Imre, 87
Napoleon, 21

national debt, 3
National Rifle Association, 9
National Science Board, 5, 159 n. 5 (ch. 1)
National Toxic Campaign Fund, 7
Native American nations, 25
Naval Ammunitions Depot, *93*, 110
Nazi death camps, 42
Nazis, 79
neo-Nazis, 42
New Jersey, 29
New York Times, 12
New Zealand, 32
Nicaragua, 25, 67, 111
The Nonviolent Activist, 159, nn. 6, 7, 8 (ch. 1)
nonviolent defense, 21
nonviolent resistance, 16, 24, *99*
Norway, 81–83
Norwegian resistance, 20, 81
Norwegian State Church, resistance of, 82
Nuremberg Law, 140

Oberhausen, 77
occupation, Soviet, 83
O'Gorman, Angie, 160 n. 2 (ch. 2)
Oklahoma City, federal building in, 12

Palestinians, 12, 44
Panama, 10, 13
Peace Media Service, 161 n. 4 (ch. 8)
Peacework, 162 n. 5 (ch. 8)
Peaceworkers (San Francisco), 115
Pentagon, 1, 6, 7, 9, 10, 11, 13, 21, 24, 124, 157
People's Liberation Army, *100*
Persian Gulf, 7
Persian Gulf War, 10, 103
Philippines, 12, *95*, *96*, *97*, 111
Pius XII, 78
Plutonium, 5
Poland, 25
police, German, 84
Portland, Oregon, 110
productivity rate, 6
Pronozin, Alexander, 115, 161 n. 4 (ch. 8)

Queens, 29
Quisling, Vidkun, 81
Quisling government, 82, 83
Quit India campaign, 109

Prague, 113; in 1968, 87
Proxmire, Senator William, 4

radio stations, German, 85
Rahman, Sheik Omar Abdul, 12
Ramo, Simon, 5
Rebber, Charles, 10
Red Square, 88
Roberts, Adam, 161 n. 5, 6 (ch. 7)
Ruhr campaign, 78
Ruhr district, 77
Russell, Bertrand, 19, 20, 21, 77, 160 n. 1 (ch. 3)
Russia. 12, 25, . *See also:* USSR

Sacramento, USS, *91, 92*
Salt Laws, 71
Salt Tax Campaign, x
salt works invasion, 37
sanctions, 67
SANE/FREEZE, 159 n. 5 (ch. 1)
satyagraha, x, xi, 15, 16, 24, 37, 67, 71–77, 80, 87, 113
satyagrahis, 71–77
Schell, Jonathan, 23, 160 n. 1 (ch. 4)
Sharp, Gene, 21, 26
Sharpeville, South Africa, 57, 58
Siegel, Lenny, 7, 159, nn. 7, 8 (ch. 1)
Sikhs, 74, 75, 76
Sivorg, 81, 83
Skodvin, Magne, 161 n. 5, 6 (ch. 7)
Sojourner's, 160 n. 14 (ch. 1)
soldiers, Chinese, *99, 100*
soldiers, Filipino, *95, 96, 97*
soldiers, German, 83
soldiers, Hungarian, 86
soldiers, Soviet, 84, 86, *101*
Somalia, 13
South Africa, xi, 15, 16, 57
South Africa and Gandhi, 15, 16

statistics. *See* Bureau of Labor Statistics; murder statistics
Stride Toward Freedom, 16
strikes, 79
swaraj (home rule), 74
Swomley, John, 10, 160 n. 16 (ch. 1)

tanks, Chinese, *98*
tanks, Filipino, *96, 97*
tanks, South Vietnamese, *90*
tanks, Soviet, *101,* 110
terrorism: domestic, 12, ; international, 12
Tiananmen Square, 42, 109, 111–114, 121, 122, 123, 138
toxic waste, 7
Trochmann, John, 13
Trocme, Andre, 80, 161 n. 4 (ch. 7)
Trondheim, 82
troop morale, 37, 64
True, Michael, 11, 160 n. 18 (ch. 1)
Truman, President Harry, 42

U2 spy plane, 35
U.S. Commerce Department, 12
U.S. Department of Defense (DOD), 3, 4, 5, 7, 8, 12, 13
U.S. military budget, 3, 4, 13
USSR (Union of Soviet Socialist Republics), 83–88
Uniform Crime Reports, 10
United Nations (UN), 12, 26, 27, 85, 87, 134
United Press International (UPI), 161 n. 1 (ch. 7)
United States, 25, 85, 157
United States federal budget, 2
University of California at Berkeley, 110
Upa River, 110, 134
Usov, Vladimir, 119

Versailles Treaty, 77
veterans, 155
veterans' benefits, 3
Vichy (French) government, 80
Vietnam, x, 7, 13, 57, 111, 157, 159 n. 9 (ch. 1)
Vietnam war, 110
violence: television, 10, ; street, 7
von Clausewitz, 26

Wall Street Journal, 11
Wallis, Jim, 160 n. 12 (ch. 1)
War Resisters League, 2, 87, 160 n. 2 (ch. 3)
Ward, Barbara, 4
Washington Post, 9
water jets, resisters, 125–128, *126, 127*
WAVE, 160 n. 10 (ch. 1)
Willson, Brian, 111, 134
WIN, 161 n. 9 (ch. 7)
Wink, Walter, 16, 17
Winter Soldiers, 155
Worcester Magazine, 160 n. 18 (ch. 1)
World Court, 26
World Trade Center, 12
World War I, 5, 19
World War II, 20, 43, 45, 80, 85, 88
World War II, resistance. *See* Denmark, France, Germany, Norway, USSR

Yeltsin, Boris, 115, 116

Zehlendorf, *89*

Page numbers for illustrations appear in italic.

About the Author

Franklin Zahn's brief military career consisted of three years of ROTC courses at California Institute of Technology and six weeks of training at an army base. In 1930 he stopped short of taking a second lieutenant's commission in the US Army Engineers Reserve Corps. He joined the Fellowship of Reconciliation in 1935, and by 1939 had started promoting antiwar meetings in his hometown of San Diego. That same year, he registered as a conscientious objector with Selective Service.

In 1942 he left his job as a mechanical engineer in the field of diesel fuel injection because of the industry's World War II connections. Later he left a teaching position at the University of Santa Clara when the college received an army contract. In 1944, he was assigned as a conscientious objector to a government Civilian Public Service Camp in Oregon where he drove a truck, cut trees, and worked in the dining hall for each unpaid 48-hour week.

Franklin Zahn committed his first act of civil disobedience when he refused a government order to transfer to another CPS camp, claiming that, although by law all camps were under civilian direction, the order was signed by an army colonel. The government refused to prosecute, but denied him the customary two weeks annual furlough. This led to his second act of civil disobedience — leaving without permission to spend Christmas with his mother and brother in San

Diego. He returned within the two-week limit and again the government refused to prosecute.

After a year in CPS camp he decided he was against not only the war but conscription itself, and he announced openly that he was "walking out." Committing his third act of civil disobedience in February 1945, he took a job in a Portland hospital as a janitor/dishwasher. In August he was convicted of desertion, a felony with the same one-to-five-year term as for a military offense. He was given six months' probation with the provision that he continue to work at the hospital. The war ended during the one week he was in jail.

Before Oregon, Zahn had worked as manager of Trabuco College in Southern California, a coeducational monastery for the study of prayer, directed by British writer/lecturer Gerald Heard. In 1946 he returned to Trabuco, but after several weeks decided he preferred social action to the contemplative life. In 1947 he bought land in Pomona, California, built his house with hand tools, devoted two hours a day to meditation, and maintained a vegetarian diet. He earned his living as a carpenter/handyman and as part-time secretary of a prison program of the American Friends Service Committee, also visiting prisoners himself. He kept his income low to avoid paying war taxes.

In the 1950s, working with the local NAACP to promote integration, he built and renovated houses which African-Americans could rent or buy in previously segregated neighborhoods. In 1952, during the Korean War, he committed a form of civil disobedience by refusing to pay the federal tax on his telephone bill and, according to the law at that time, lost his phone service. In 1962 he was one of three nuclear protesters arrested aboard *Everyman II* in the forbidden test zone surrounding Johnston Island, for which he was held in a Honolulu jail for eighteen days and fined $400. This fifth act of civil disobedience, although only a misdemeanor, proved to be his most newsworthy.

He spent most of 1963–64 in India as a volunteer for a self-help housing project, "Shelters for the Shelterless," FOR's peace alternative to building backyard bomb shelters. He spoke to Indian audiences on the subject of how Martin Luther King, Jr. was applying Gandhi's nonviolent techniques in the American civil rights campaign. Home in Pomona, he wrote a novel describing how King's followers could defend the United States against an armed invasion — his first of several unpublished books on nonviolent national defense.

During the Vietnam War he organized the Southern California branch of a taxpayers' suit against the federal government, claiming the increased phone tax to support the war was illegal because the undeclared war was itself illegal. He collected over $10,000 in unpaid phone taxes from some 400 subscribers, but both suits in California were lost. In 1972, in a symbolic blockade of a munitions ship leaving Seal Beach Naval Weapons Station, he was arrested in a wet suit, and for this sixth act of civil disobedience he spent one day in Orange County Jail.

Franklin Zahn's autobiography, *Deserter from Violence: Experiments with Gandhi's Truth*, was published in 1984. Zahn died on June 3, 1996.